CRADLE OF CONSERVATION

ALLEN DIETERICH-WARD

CRADLE OF CONSERVATION

AN ENVIRONMENTAL HISTORY OF PENNSYLVANIA

THE PENNSYLVANIA
HISTORICAL
ASSOCIATION

TEMPLE UNIVERSITY PRESS
Philadelphia | Rome | Tokyo

Temple University Press
Philadelphia, Pennsylvania 19122
tupress.temple.edu

Library of Congress Cataloging-in-Publication Data

Names: Dieterich-Ward, Allen, author.
Title: Cradle of conservation : an environmental history of Pennsylvania /
  Allen Dieterich-Ward.
Other titles: Pennsylvania history studies.
Description: Philadelphia : Temple University Press, 2024. | Series:
  Pennsylvania history series | Includes bibliographical references and
  index. | Summary: "A survey of Pennsylvania's environmental history from
  pre-colonial and colonial eras through to the development of industrial
  and post-industrial society"— Provided by publisher.
Identifiers: LCCN 2024000276 (print) | LCCN 2024000277 (ebook) | ISBN
  9781932304381 (paperback) | ISBN 9781932304428 (pdf)
Subjects: LCSH: Human ecology—Pennsylvania—History. | Nature
  conservation—Pennsylvania—History. | Nature—Effect of human beings
  on—Pennsylvania—History. | Pennsylvania—Environmental conditions.
Classification: LCC GF13.3.P46 D54 2024 (print) | LCC GF13.3.P46 (ebook)
  | DDC 304.209748—dc23/eng/20240514
LC record available at https://lccn.loc.gov/2024000276
LC ebook record available at https://lccn.loc.gov/2024000277

Printed in the United States of America

9 8 7 6 5 4 3 2

CONTENTS

EDITOR'S FOREWORD

David Witwer

O N BEHALF OF THE MEMBERS and officers of the Pennsylvania Historical Association (PHA), I am pleased to introduce the fifth book in the newest generation of the Pennsylvania History Series (PHS), a series that has grown out of a partnership formed with Temple University Press in 2016. This book series reflects the PHA's core mission to advocate and advance knowledge about the history and culture of Pennsylvania and the Mid-Atlantic region. With this series, the PHA seeks to put forward relevant historical scholarship of the highest caliber and to make that scholarship available in a form that is both compact and accessible. The authors of the books in this series are published experts in their fields, but they are also seasoned teachers. They are committed to producing volumes on Pennsylvania history that will meet classroom needs and that will also engage a more general audience.

Allen Dieterich-Ward exemplifies this combination of qualities. A committed teacher who now serves as director of The Graduate School at Shippensburg University, Allen is also a widely respected scholar. His book, *Beyond Rust: Metropolitan Pittsburgh and the Fate of Industrial America* (2016), won the Arline Custer Memorial Award for Best Book on Mid-Atlantic History. In addition, he is the author or coauthor of a series of journal articles on environmental history in Pennsylvania. The current volume reflects his confident command of this scholarship, but it also demonstrates his commitment to produce a highly readable text that provides a fascinating introduction to the state's environmental history. In a text that spans chronologically from the precolonial era to the present, Allen covers a range of issues, all the while offering narrative details that connect the reader with compelling individual stories. His text particularly emphasizes working landscapes, a concept that refers to how the state's environment has always reflected the evolving impact of human activity. In this way, his environmental history of Pennsylvania considers not the just state's wilderness and rural areas, but also its urban and industrial centers. His book also traces the history of the environmental movement, which emerged in response to the negative effects that industrial development was having on the state's working landscapes.

I express my appreciation to the peer reviewers and the PHS editorial board who provided feedback and guidance as this manuscript evolved into its final form. Support from the PHA Council makes this series possible. Working with the excellent staff at Temple University Press has been both an honor and a pleasure. The Pennsylvania Parks and Forests Foundation provided financial support for the color map of Pennsylvania's major river basins in Chapter 1. Finally, I acknowledge the generous assistance that Allen himself provided to me as I took over from him and assumed the new role as solo editor of this series.

ACKNOWLEDGMENTS

THE SEED FOR THIS BOOK was planted more than a decade ago when Paul Douglas Newman, then editor of the journal *Pennsylvania History*, encouraged me to develop a special issue on environmental history. That was an exciting offer for an assistant professor with only one published article, and I remain grateful that David Hsiung of Juniata College agreed to split the responsibility. As we collected essays and shepherded the volume toward publication, my involvement with the South Mountain Partnership led me to a group of retired and current state officials, nonprofit leaders, and academics that eventually became the Pennsylvania Conservation Heritage Project (PCHP). Under the inspired leadership of Brenda Barrett and Wayne Kober, the PCHP collected oral histories; developed a timeline, bibliography, and website; and partnered with WITF Media on a series of moving documentaries detailing the state's conservation and environmental movements. *Cradle of Conservation* is the next iteration of this ongoing project, and I am grateful to everyone who has lent their time helping tell this story.

The most difficult part of writing this book was the necessity of leaving out so much to maintain the emphasis of the Pennsylvania History Series on brevity and readability. I am especially thankful that David Witwer, the series editor, allowed me to squeak in at the maximum word count, then top it off with a bunch of images. Suggestions by my old friend David Hsiung greatly improved the first chapter, and careful full manuscript reads by Brian Black, John Bloom, Marci Mowery, and David Stradling shaped extensive revisions. Thoughtful feedback from editorial board members enabled a final polish that would not have been achieved otherwise. I hope they are all pleased with the results. The images were collected by Linda Ries, herself one of the commonwealth's great treasures, who called in multiple favors to access photographs held by the Pennsylvania State Archives, which was closed for a move throughout much of 2023.

I completed the initial manuscript thanks to a sabbatical provided by Shippensburg University and funded by my students and the Pennsylvania taxpayers who support our great State System of Higher Education. Some of the book's key ideas, particularly those related to working landscapes, emerged during invited talks at the Pennsylvania Historical Association conference; at Mansfield, Lock Haven, and Chatham universities and the McGowan Center for Ethics and Social Responsibility at King's College; and at the annual meeting of the Land and Water Conservation Fund. I also thank several former graduate students, especially Chad Crumrine, Christine Hegarty, and Martha Moon-Renton, whose ideas about environmental history made their way into the volume. Finally, as always, I owe the deepest debt to my wife, Amanda, with whom I share a life (and now a farm) at the base of South Mountain in the Great Valley of the Appalachians along with our beloved herd of six cats and three horses.

CRADLE OF CONSERVATION

INTRODUCTION

Nature's Commonwealth

A S RALPH BROCK ROSE to give his presentation "Fertilizers for Renewing Nursery Soils," the twenty-five-year-old forester had reasons to be proud of his accomplishments. Two years earlier, in 1906, he had been part of the first graduating class at the Pennsylvania State Forest Academy, which was among the nation's earliest forestry schools. A native of West Chester, Brock had achieved academic success that attracted the attention of Dr. Joseph Rothrock, a botanist at the University of Pennsylvania and the state's first forestry commissioner, who secured the young man's appointment as a student forester. His skills must have been evident to everyone around him, because even before graduation Brock began serving as student superintendent of the school's tree nursery, a position he then formally assumed after finishing his studies. In early March 1908, Rothrock's successor, Robert S. Conklin, gathered the first two graduating classes along with the four other members of the State Forestry Reservation Commission for an inaugural convention of Pennsylvania foresters, and it was here that Brock was about to speak.[1]

The offices of the seven-year-old Department of Forestry were in Pennsylvania's magnificent new beaux arts–style State Capitol building. When Brock and his fellow foresters arrived that morning, they would have walked up the steps on which President Theodore Roosevelt, himself a well-known conservation advocate, had given a speech dedicating a building he described as "the handsomest state capitol I have ever seen." "Pennsylvania's soil is historic," Roosevelt declared in an address that praised the commonwealth's role in the Seven Years' War, American Revolution, and Civil War, before turning to a fiery Progressive-era denunciation of corporate greed and political graft and a narrow interpretation of federal power. The massive bronze doors of the Capitol's western entrance would have had special significance to Brock and his contemporaries with their depiction not only of William Penn, the Declaration of Independence, and the U.S. Constitution but also of the mining and agriculture that, along with forests, defined the state's environmental history. As they entered the building and walked toward their meeting room, Moravian tiles on the rotunda and hallway floors evoked natural and industrial history with colorful depictions of foxes, turkeys, cows, and bears, along with a spinning wheel, beer mug, and Conestoga wagon.[2]

It is fitting, then, that this story of Pennsylvania as the figurative "cradle of conservation" begins here with Ralph Brock and his very real nursery at the dawn of the conservation era. No one recorded their impressions of Brock's presentation or the subsequent discussion of what were rather mundane and technical matters related to seedling propagation. The circumstances and location of his talk, however, allow us to begin exploring a few key ideas that will shape the rest of this book. While most of the people in the room were White men, Brock was Black; indeed, he was the first African American formally trained as a forester. Also present was Mira Lloyd Dock, the first woman in the world to serve on a forestry commission and the first in Pennsylvania to hold a statewide office. The prominent position of these two figures at such an important moment highlights the fascinating, complex, and often untold stories of the state's environmental history (Figure I.1).

Though I did start by talking about forestry, by now it should be clear that this book is not just about trees. Environmental history encompasses all the myriad interactions between and among humans and the rest of the nonhuman world across time. In general, we can divide this into three broad categories for exploration. First, how does the rest of the nonhuman world shape our history? Second, how have human actions shaped our environment in ways that often rebounded to cause other changes in society? Finally, how have we thought about the nonhuman world, and how have patterns in those thoughts affected actions? When conceived in such broad terms, environmental history can potentially touch on virtually every aspect of the human experience and the world around us. *Cradle of Conservation* does not attempt to address comprehensively every way in which humans interacted with the rest of nature throughout the state's history. While this is the first to tackle the environmental history of the whole commonwealth, there are plenty of excellent regional and thematic studies on which to draw. Instead, my goal is

Figure I.1 Pennsylvania state foresters, 1908. With Mira Lloyd Dock, Ralph Brock, and Joseph T. Rothrock in Rothrock's office, State Capitol building. (Courtesy: Franklin County Historical Society.)

to provide an introductory overview of key ideas, events, places, and people that will leave readers, like Ralph Brock's seedlings, firmly rooted in the rich soil of Pennsylvania's history and thirsting to learn more.[3]

While the term *nature* is often used as shorthand to refer to those elements of the world distinct from human "culture," the reality, of course, is that the two are always inextricably linked. After all, paving over a forest to create a freeway does not remove natural processes from the equation; it merely changes them into different forms, with black bears and wolves giving way to automobiles as apex predators, for example.[4] Throughout the book I use the concept of working landscapes to emphasize the ways in which the natural world and human culture combine within integrated environments. The "landscape" part of the concept indicates a cohesive, connected area of varying size, while "working" suggests the human involvement that has altered that area in some fundamental way to serve a social need. There are all sorts of working landscapes throughout Pennsylvania's history—barns, cornfields, and horse-drawn implements in eighteenth-century Lancaster County;

immense forests, smoke from charcoal fires, and the clank of iron furnaces in nineteenth-century Pittsburgh; and diesel fumes, honking horns, and truck stops on the twentieth century Pennsylvania Turnpike. As societal needs and cultural values evolved over time, so, too, did the ways in which human activities manifested as changes in the physical environment. Each succeeding generation was not presented with a blank slate of unblemished green space but, instead, found its activities constrained by its ancestors' use (and abuse) of the environment.[5]

The working landscapes of the Mid-Atlantic underscore just how porous the boundaries are between nature and culture. Native Americans have occupied this area for at least ten thousand years and began integrating agriculture into their hunting-and-gathering lifestyle more than a thousand years ago. When Europeans began arriving on the coast, they described the forested woodlands as parklike, which they often interpreted as acts of God rather than recognizing the role of indigenous people in using fire to clear the undergrowth and provide nutrients for their crops. European diseases decimated Native Americans even as Eurasian animals, from honeybees to horses, pigs, and cows, reordered existing ecosystems. European settler colonialism brought eastern North America into a transatlantic marketplace that increasingly drove environmental change. Port cities of New York, Wilmington, and Philadelphia developed agricultural hinterlands that used human, ox, and horsepower to translate water, soil, and sunlight into calories that powered an empire and then, following the American Revolution, an imperial republic. The combination of fertile soils with a climate too cool for growing tobacco (in large quantities) and cotton attracted large numbers of poor Europeans whose descendants valorized free labor as they grudgingly emancipated enslaved people of African descent. The region served as the nation's population center, breadbasket, and workshop as transportation improvements, from turnpikes to canals and, finally, railroads, prompted fires of industrialization fed by untold acres of trees and tons of coal.

Ecosystems are regional in scale and rarely align with political boundaries, but approaching environmental history at the state level provides insight into how political and environmental contexts combine to shape important historical patterns. By the mid-nineteenth century, the degradation of industrial and urban environments increasingly concerned many residents. The national movement to conserve natural resources first gained traction among some of the wealthy civic leaders of Philadelphia and New York City whose families had made their fortunes from extraction: hence, the term *cradle of conservation*. Indeed, the Hudson River School of landscape painting that helped shape a more positive view of nonhuman nature and thus provided the cultural underpinnings for conservationism arguably originated along the banks of the Schuylkill River in Philadelphia, where the artist Thomas Cole began his professional career in the early 1820s. However, Philadelphia elites did not develop the same dominance over state politics enjoyed by New Yorkers, who moved in 1885 to assert control over a vast swath of the Catskill and Adirondack mountains to protect their water supply. Instead, Pennsylvania remained more balanced in terms of rural and urban interests, so conservationists here had to build a more diverse political consensus around a system of statewide forest reserves established in 1893.

Pennsylvania differed from New York and the rest of the Mid-Atlantic in one other crucial way: its wealth of carbon resources. Coal, oil, and natural gas transformed the state's working landscapes, setting the stage for an industrial revolution in the late nineteenth century and a legacy of abandoned wells with which we are still dealing. The vertical integration of industrial corporations made cities such as Pittsburgh, Johnstown, and Bethlehem both symbols of economic might and, by the mid-twentieth century, cautionary tales of how the fouling of air, water, and land could transform working landscapes from sources of wealth into zones of sacrifice. Like the burning of Cleveland's Cuyahoga River and Santa Barbara's oil spill, the infamous Donora Smog in 1948 endures as a symbol of hubris that led eventually to the rise of the environmental movement and, for Pennsylvanians, the 1971 constitutional amendment that ensures every resident the "right to clean air, pure water, and to the preservation of the natural, scenic, historic and esthetic values of the environment."[6] As Pennsylvanians continue to grapple with the regulatory balance between natural resource consumption and conservation, the crisis of global warming adds urgency to viewing our history through an environmental lens. Even as many residents proved willing to embrace an ethic linking their own health and well-being to the rest of the natural world, since the 1970s an antienvironmental movement that questions additional regulation has gained momentum in the wake of deindustrialization. This has proved especially contentious in tandem with demands for "environmental justice"—an acknowledgment that discrimination based on race, class, and other social characteristics has always shaped access to environmental amenities. The scientific consensus about the need to decrease the burning of fossil fuels has done little to dampen a new energy boom in the natural-gas fields of the state's north and west. Unlike in New York, which effectively banned the high-volume hydraulic fracturing technology necessary to extract shale gas beginning in 2015, the relative power of the state's energy-producing regions forced a more limited approach to environmental politics. In the end, however, it is this very ambivalence toward environmental protection, particularly when it seems to conflict with economic opportunity, that makes Pennsylvania an ideal case study. Tracing the evolution of the nation's cradle of conservation as it has come to face an uncertain future is the subject of the pages that follow.

1

CREATING PENN'S WOODS

WHEN HIS DOG dug out a groundhog burrow in 1955, little did Arthur Miller know that the ancient artifacts he uncovered would point the way to one of the most important archaeological finds of the twentieth century. Meadowcroft Rockshelter, carved by nature from a bluff overlooking a tributary of the Ohio River twenty-five miles southwest of Pittsburgh, challenged long-held assumptions about the hemisphere's earliest human settlements. The archaeologist James Adovasio began excavating the site in the mid-1970s when the prevailing consensus was that the first human society in the Americas, known as the Clovis culture, appeared around 13,200 to 12,900 years ago. Consequently, Meadowcroft's initial radiocarbon dating, which indicated occupation beginning sixteen thousand and possibly as early as nineteen thousand years ago, set off furious debate. In the more than forty years since, excavation of other pre-Clovis sites, particularly Monte Verde in Chile and Saltville in Virginia, has reinforced this earlier timeline, as well as the significance of the Pennsylvania site itself.[1]

During the long period Meadowcroft depicts, Native American cultures developed and diversified in countless ways as they created the state's first working landscapes. European colonists had to adapt traditional land-use behavior to the lived reality of their new homes, as well, and adopted certain indigenous agricultural practices. Conversely, the introduction of plants, animals, and microbes from Eurasia, known as the Columbian exchange, had such profound effects that Native Americans, too, faced a new world that undermined long-standing social practices. The creation of a transatlantic market economy linked exploitation of local working landscapes to demands of distant empires and populations and increasingly drove environmental change. By the Revolutionary War, Pennsylvania was the leading producer in the Americas of both wheat and iron as its fields and factories formed the new nation's environmental keystone.

First Pennsylvanians

A common element among origin stories of the Haudenosaunee (Iroquoian-speaking) and Lenape (Algonquin-speaking) peoples of the area that became Pennsylvania was the tale of Turtle and Muskrat. In one version, a primeval being, sometimes called Sky Woman, fell from a realm above the sky toward the great water below, and Turtle agreed to provide a resting place on his back. Needing earth for her to walk on, Otter and Beaver tried many times to reach the lake's bottom but were unsuccessful. Finally, Muskrat dove and stayed down for a very long time. Resurfacing, he spat a mouthful of mud onto Turtle's back and thus created a home for Sky Woman. These myths, perhaps, memorialized the retreat of the region's last glaciers by about 10,600 BCE. The northern tier remained a frozen tundra, but fir and spruce forests intermixed with open grasslands dominated farther south, grazed by bison, deer, elk, caribou, moose, and muskox. In an early example of human-induced environmental change, larger animals, such as mastodon and mammoth, coexisted with Paleoamericans before climate-induced habitat loss and hunting caused their extinction. Forests, open meadows, and wetlands that provided a more life-sustaining variety of plant and animal resources spread along the seacoast, far east of the present-day shore.[2]

A second series of creation myths describe Sky Mother's grandson, known as the Good Twin or Sky-Grasper, who, with the aid of Turtle (his father), improved the world by making various animals that were good for food; rivers that eased travel by canoeing; and, finally, mortal humans. During a long period of climate change, these indigenous cultures developed and diversified in countless ways by adapting to their landscapes. Around 8000 BCE, rising seas began to create the modern shoreline, and glacial runoff eventually left behind fertile stream terraces and small islands that attracted human settlement. As rivers assumed their present form, they established a lasting geographical orientation linking the Delaware and Chesapeake bays with today's upstate New York via the Susquehanna and Delaware river basins (Figure 1.1). In contrast, the Allegheny River, separated by ridges and valleys of the Appalachian Mountains, looked west toward the Ohio and Mississippi river systems. Over many centuries, a succession of forests spread northward, eventually leaving a mix of pine, spruce, chestnut, hemlock, oak, and hickory that provided food for deer and other animals, as well as for the humans who hunted them. The rivers, too, teemed with fish and fowl, particularly during migratory seasons and spring spawning runs of saltwater herring, shad, and other species headed upstream.[3]

At every turn, Good Twin's brother, Evil Twin, and Sky Mother herself sought to undo the blessings Sky-Grasper tried to provide. Evil Twin made rivers crooked and placed obstacles to navigation and made animals dangerous and unwilling to give themselves to humans as food. Good Twin persisted and taught mortals the proper ceremonies, sometimes involving the smoking of tobacco, to keep harm at bay, offer thanksgiving, and appease spirits of the world around them. The people of Pennsylvania, especially those living east of the Appalachians, remained largely isolated from growing civilizations of the Mississippi and Ohio river valleys; nevertheless, innovations slowly made their way in. The proliferation of axes, adzes, and other woodworking tools suggests that residents were making dugout canoes, clearing trees, and cutting firewood, while cooking pots, mortars and pestles, fishnet anchors, and carefully dug storage pits indicate increasing sophistication in food acquisition and preparation. Initially, local groups probably consisted of twenty-five to fifty members who gathered and hunted in a stream drainage or similar area of around five hundred square miles. "We lived off of the bounty of the forest, the bounty of the rivers, and the bounty of the oceans," explained the Lenape historian Curtis Zunigha. "And it was a holistic lifestyle, in the sense that all things had a living spirit. And we were given a way of life, to live and balance in harmony with those spirits."[4]

Perhaps Good Twin's greatest gift was the secret of agriculture: the cultivation of maize and other crops. However, the succulent ears originally introduced to humans were tainted by the actions of Sky Mother, who threw ashes into the cooking pot and decreed henceforth maize must be parched and ground before it could be eaten. By the first century CE, early adoptions of wild rice and grasses such as goosefoot and pigweed were joined by sunflowers that were widely cultivated in the Ohio Valley. The global warming trend known as the Medieval Optimum—an increase of a few degrees in average annual temperature in the Northern Hemisphere that lasted from about 900 CE until the mid-1300s—for the first time allowed many indigenous people to rely on cultivated plants for a major portion of their diet. While the shift to agriculture played out somewhat differently in various parts of the region, as the creation story suggests, the core innovation was the adoption of maize, beans, and squash. Beans had been grown for thousands of years in Central America and for centuries in southwestern North America, but they were

PENNSYLVANIA'S MAJOR RIVER BASINS

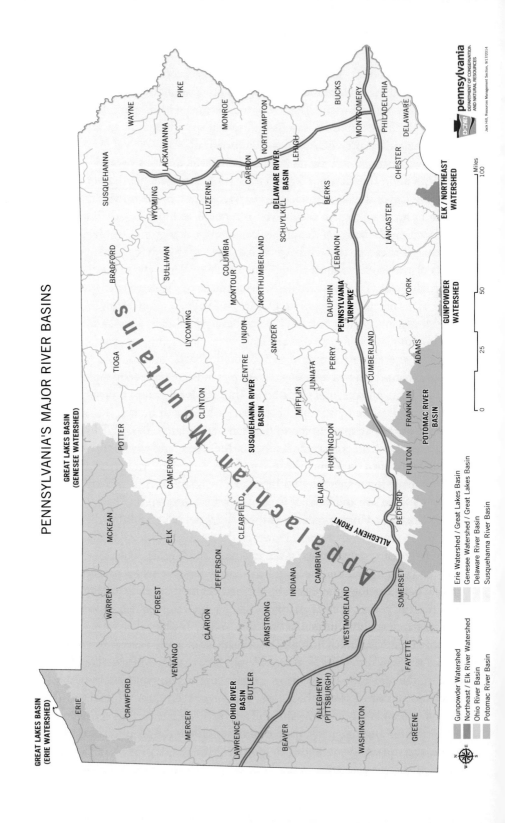

GREAT LAKES BASIN
(ERIE WATERSHED)

GREAT LAKES BASIN
(GENESEE WATERSHED)

DELAWARE RIVER BASIN

SUSQUEHANNA RIVER BASIN

PENNSYLVANIA TURNPIKE

POTOMAC RIVER BASIN

LAWRENCE OHIO RIVER BASIN (PITTSBURGH)

ALLEGHENY FRONT

Appalachian Mountains

ELK / NORTHEAST WATERSHED

GUNPOWDER WATERSHED

Counties: ERIE, CRAWFORD, WARREN, MCKEAN, POTTER, TIOGA, BRADFORD, SUSQUEHANNA, WAYNE, PIKE, MONROE, LACKAWANNA, WYOMING, SULLIVAN, LYCOMING, CAMERON, ELK, FOREST, VENANGO, MERCER, BEAVER, LAWRENCE, BUTLER, CLARION, JEFFERSON, CLEARFIELD, CENTRE, CLINTON, UNION, MONTOUR, COLUMBIA, LUZERNE, CARBON, NORTHAMPTON, LEHIGH, BERKS, SCHUYLKILL, NORTHUMBERLAND, SNYDER, MIFFLIN, JUNIATA, PERRY, DAUPHIN, LEBANON, LANCASTER, BUCKS, MONTGOMERY, PHILADELPHIA, DELAWARE, CHESTER, YORK, ADAMS, CUMBERLAND, FRANKLIN, FULTON, BEDFORD, HUNTINGDON, BLAIR, CAMBRIA, INDIANA, ARMSTRONG, WESTMORELAND, ALLEGHENY, WASHINGTON, GREENE, FAYETTE, SOMERSET

Legend

Gunpowder Watershed

Northeast / Elk River Watershed

Ohio River Basin

Potomac River Basin

Erie Watershed / Great Lakes Basin

Genesee Watershed / Great Lakes Basin

Delaware River Basin

Susquehanna River Basin

Miles
0   25   50   100

pennsylvania
DEPARTMENT OF CONSERVATION AND NATURAL RESOURCES

Jack Hill, Resources Management Section, 9/17/2014

apparently not successfully adapted to eastern North American until the Medieval Optimum. Legumes were central to unlocking the potential of maize, which by itself is low in nutritional value but in combination provides a protein-rich diet. The third "sister," squash, grew symbiotically with the rest of this triad, crowding out weeds and retaining moisture while the cornstalks provided support for the soil-replenishing beans.[5]

By about 1500 CE, indigenous populations may have risen to ten times their pre-horticultural numbers as, over time, a period of historical change rooted in the adoption of agriculture created distinct working landscapes dominated by different collections of social groups in each of Pennsylvania's three main river systems. Among the Monongahela in the southwest, the Haudenosaunee and the Susquehannock in the north and center, and the Algonquian-speaking Munsee and Lenape in the east, the growing significance of crops encouraged communities to remain in one area for longer periods and increased the economic and social power of the women who grew them. Hunting and fishing remained important activities primarily for men, with the result that, as women focused more on tending crops, villages became their provinces for many months of the year. This can be seen in the stress markers left on bones from repetitive tasks and the relatively lower number of male remains found in archaeological digs, suggesting that boys and men often died away from villages.[6]

Agriculture also increased workloads within and warfare among groups as population growth during good years increased the possibility for starvation and strife following inevitable bad harvests, particularly as the Medieval Optimum gave way to a period of cooler weather. This era of strife rooted in environmental change provided the setting for the origin story of the Five Nations of the Haudenosaunee—literally, "the whole house." "Everywhere there was peril and everywhere mourning," one version of the tale reported. "Feuds with outer nations, feuds with brother nations, feuds of sister towns and feuds of families and of clans made every warrior a stealthy man who liked to kill." Driven mad by the death of his daughters, a man called Hiawatha wandered into the forest, where he encountered the otherworldly Deganawidah, the Peacemaker, perhaps a reincarnation of the Good Twin, who taught him new rituals that eased grief, cleared the mind, and held the promise of creating greater social solidarity among adherents. As Peacemaker and Hiawatha spread their gospel, they encountered Tadadaho, a powerful sor-

---

(facing page) **Figure 1.1** Major river basins of Pennsylvania. (Courtesy: Pennsylvania Department of Conservation and Natural Resources.)

cerer so filled with rage that his hair had become a tangled mass of snakes. Hiawatha, whose name means "he who combs," demonstrated the power of the new spiritual principles by smoothing the hair of Tadadaho, who subsequently joined with Hiawatha, Peacemaker, and their followers in forming a powerful confederacy that would dominate the region for more than two hundred years.[7]

Beyond the cultural and social realms, the adoption of agriculture among the first Pennsylvanians had significant environmental consequences. Despite the efficiency of women's practices, domesticated crops eventually reduced soil nutrients, and new fields further from village centers had to be cleared of trees. At the same time, growing communities needed wood and vegetable fibers to make everything from baskets to houses. These two trends gradually depleted significant portions of nearby forests. Within villages, wooden and bark construction materials gradually rotted; waste pits expanded; and insects and other pests invaded storage pits. After about two decades, a town site outlived its usefulness, and the community moved on, generally to a site a few miles away. At any given time, then, a single community needed not only its current site and surrounding farmland, but also enough land and timber for future sites, a variety of camps for fishing and fowling, sufficient hunting ground, and the areas where prior village sites were going through the process of replenishing. Native peoples further shaped their environment through the extensive and varied use of fire. Communities used controlled burns to clear fields for agriculture, with the ash providing the added benefit of restoring nutrients to the soil. Fire may have also encouraged the spread of hickory, walnut, and other flame-resistant nut trees that provided important sources of protein.[8]

What Europeans were to regard as empty countryside with only a few widely scattered villages was therefore actually a spiritually rich and actively managed working landscape. By the early 1670s, the English had defeated rival Swedish and Dutch colonies along the Atlantic coast, and in 1681, King Charles II granted the territory that would become Pennsylvania and Delaware to William Penn. While Penn had converted to the pacifist Quaker tradition, the bequest was intended to settle a debt to his father, an admiral, and the area covered by the charter was named "Pennsylvania" in the elder Penn's honor—a combination of the family surname and the Latin *sylvan*, or woods—so, literally, "Penn's Woods." The arrival of Europeans resulted in two types of profound changes to the North American environment. First was what historians call the Columbian exchange—the extensive and ongoing transfer of plants, animals, and microbes between the Eastern and Western hemispheres. The significance of the introduction of domestic livestock and grains and of honeybees, earthworms, rodents, and myriad other items cannot be understated. What was to be a "New World" for Europeans was every bit as new to the indigenous inhabitants of Pennsylvania, both human and nonhuman. Eurasian diseases eventually wiped out up to 90 percent of the Native American population, and the chestnut blight, for example, wrought devastation on a species that may once have accounted for one in four trees in Pennsylvania forests. The social crisis caused by epidemic disease coupled with rivalries over access to European trade goods led to an arms race, known as the Beaver Wars, fueled by brass and iron arrowheads that reshuffled settlement patterns among Iroquoian- and Algonquian-speaking peoples from the Delaware Valley to the eastern Great Lakes.[9]

The cultural values of Europeans related to the environment were also quite different from those of the first Pennsylvanians. While it is important not to romanticize or overly generalize regarding Native Americans' environmental ethic, their origin myths make clear spiritual beliefs that incorporated nature to a much greater extent than Christianity. The notion of reciprocity taught in the creation stories by the Good Twin—that through appropriate rituals animals would agree to give their bodies for food or winds might restrain themselves to allow a canoe passage across a lake—extended to the human realm. Property rights, for example, rested much more on practical need or usage than on abstract notions of ownership, and community leaders held their positions through their ability to provide goods to others rather than accumulation for themselves. Indeed, the Good Twin assigned roles to various groups of people, or clans, named after animals, to keep the ceremonies that would appease the spirits that populated the world around them. The introduction of a transatlantic market that assigned high value to certain goods, such as beaver pelts, reduced community constraints on overhunting, brought a variety of indigenous species to the brink of extinction, and induced changes that rippled throughout ecosystems.[10]

First encounters between Penn's colonists and the Lenape people have been mythologized in works such as Benjamin West's *Penn's Treaty with the Indians* (1772–1773) and Edward Hicks's *The Peaceable Kingdom* (1833), but the pacifism and utopianism of the Quakers did have real significance in tempering their relations with both Native people and the natural world. Further, the lower population numbers, dispersed community structure, and reliance on indigenous expertise in obtaining valuable commodities in North America, such as trapping for pelts, meant that British colonists were forced to establish more equitable, market-based relationships with Native Americans, especially compared with the Spanish. A good example of this is Conrad Weiser, a German-born farmer, tanner, and politician who gained significant status as an interpreter in the Pennsylvania backcountry after living among the Mohawk (one of the Five Nations of the Haudenosaunee) when he was sixteen. Weiser subsequently participated in every major treaty between the colonial government and Native officials from 1731 to his death in 1760.[11]

Nevertheless, Penn's utopian experiment was tempered by the worldly demands of profit, which required the acquisition, division, and sale of land to owners who expected to be able to exploit their property for private gain. Indeed, Penn's 1681 guidance "that, in clearing the ground, care be taken to leave one acre of trees for every five acres cleared, especially to preserve oak and mulberries, for silk and shipping," which has been widely pointed to as emblematic of a nascent environmentalism, is equally important in understanding the proprietor's commercial imperative. This commodification of the landscape had enormous consequences. By 1685, the English had taken leadership over existing Dutch settlements, such as New Castle (New Amstel), and established new communities along the Delaware River, including Philadelphia, which was duly purchased from the Lenape people according to European customs. Penn's liberal economic and religious policies attracted a remarkable diversity of ethnic and religious groups, including German-, Dutch-, French-, and Swedish-speakers, as well as English-speakers. Penn and, later, his wife and then their sons struggled to affirm their own title to the land in face of competing claims even as they recruited immigrants that they expected would provide quitrents. This resulted in a haphazard process of conquest marked by squatting and often informal property boundaries that sparked conflict both between and among various Native and European groups. Waves of successive land seizures ensued, including the infamous 1737 "Walking Purchase," which eventually expanded the colony's formal boundary to the Great Valley of the Appalachians west of the Susquehanna River.[12]

"The Best Poor Man's Country"

Cornwall Furnace in Lebanon County tells the story of the charcoal-burning iron furnaces that undergirded the state's initial rise as an industrial powerhouse in the eighteenth century. It is the only intact charcoal furnace of its kind anywhere in the Americas, which means that unlike the remnant stone stacks dotted throughout the Mid-Atlantic, all the furnace and foundry equipment, offices and outbuildings, and even worker's homes are still there to memorialize an iconic working landscape. Perhaps even more striking than the giant mechanical hammer in the forge are thousands of acres of former ore banks that were actively mined from 1742 until Hurricane Agnes flooded the remaining operations in 1972. The five hundred-foot-deep min-

Figure 1.2 Old charcoal furnace, Cornwall, Pennsylvania, ca. 1935. (Courtesy: Library of Congress, Prints and Photographs Division.)

ing scar is visible from Boyd Street, but the adjacent State Game Lands provide hikers with glimpses of waste rock and the foundations of mine buildings slowly being reclaimed by trees.[13]

European colonists understood that their ability to be self-sufficient required finding marketable commodities, such as the iron products made at Cornwall Furnace (Figure 1.2) or the foodstuffs and tanned hides of the Conrad Weiser farmstead, with which to trade for goods they needed to live and to live well. As a result, the most significant cultural innovation driving environmental change in the eighteenth century was the introduction of a transatlantic market economy. Almost all of Penn's Woods was originally forested, so the first order of business for those interested in agriculture and manufacturing alike was to clear the land. Farming in what is now southeastern Pennsylvania initially featured "mixed" and "extensive" land use, meaning that colonists generally cleared more land for crops rather than trying to increase yields in existing fields. Instead of continuous cultivation using the labor-intensive management techniques of the well-established agricultural communities they left behind, colonial farmers, like the indigenous peoples they dispossessed, left fields fallow whenever yields began to decline. Colonists also adopted "Indian corn" (maize), which grew quickly, required relatively little attention, tolerated semi-cleared fields, and provided excellent fodder for humans and animals. The introduction of domesticated livestock—horses, cattle, pigs, sheep, ducks, goats, geese, and chickens—had major environmental effects not only in terms of how much land could be cleared for crop production but also in the amount of land that needed to be dedicated to feeding the livestock.[14]

In contrast to the bucolic ideal of the colonial farm, the emerging agricultural landscape in most places was, in the words of the historian Sally McMurry, "scruffy and unkempt," with a combination of stump-filled fields, woods, lowland meadows created by drainage ditches, and fallow grounds slowly returning to a semi-natural state surrounding log homes, barns, and sheds. Establishing farms in a vast forest, under unfamiliar climactic conditions and with limited labor resources, meant that using land and moving on made more sense than the intensive practices they knew from their homelands. After all, the land was initially productive enough without recycling manure, so they let animals roam and forage for themselves. Yields in the early eighteenth century were as low as ten bushels per acre, and on a one hundred-plus acre farm with about thirty acres cleared, the most important market commodity, wheat, was planted on only about ten acres. Farmers practiced a mixed agriculture that included grains, such as oats, rye, and barley (for beer); root vegetables; cabbage; flax (for both food and linen) and hemp. They also raised and sold small numbers of cattle, sheep, swine, horses, and poultry, along with the associated products of pork, beef, mutton, tallow, eggs, milk, and butter.[15]

The fact that only a relatively small portion of eighteenth-century Pennsylvania farms were planted in crops destined for transatlantic markets can be misleading as to their overall importance. Periodic crop failures and burgeoning populations in Europe and the West Indies meant that by the eve of the American Revolution, Pennsylvanians had buyers for a variety of products, especially wheat. In 1770, a good year, the export value of the colony's wheat and wheat flour dwarfed corn, meat, and flaxseed combined. By 1790, eight three- and four-story mills clustered along the lower Brandywine River to prepare grain for export. In far western Cumberland County, dozens of smaller local mills proliferated along the Conodoguinet, Yellow Breeches, and Conococheague creeks, along with some of their larger tributaries. Of course, colonists demanded new roads be made to get goods to market, and this required wagons and horses, which, in turn, necessitated skilled labor, wood, iron, and acres upon acres of hay. The Lancaster-Philadelphia turnpike was the first paved highway in America, and on a visit to the area in the

1770s, the French-turned-British American farmer Hector St. John de Crève-coeur observed through the voice of a companion from the Hebrides that the horses from "several large Lancaster six-horse wagons . . . would eat all the grass of our island!"[16]

The booming wheat crop also served as the basis for industrial development, especially ironmaking, which similarly created distinct working landscapes. Iron products were indispensable for Europeans and formed a significant part of trade both between and among colonists and Native Americans. In a 1681 promotional tract, William Penn had alluded to iron as one of the products "the country is thought capable of," and the raw materials were readily available—iron ore, limestone for removing impurities, and hardwood forests for charcoal. Colonial entrepreneurs, known as iron masters, built smelting furnaces near ore deposits, which were generally close to the surface and quarried via large pits or trenches that rarely exceeded a depth of forty feet. Thomas Rutter, a trained blacksmith, built Pennsylvania's first charcoal blast furnace on Matawny Creek near Pottstown in 1720, with the industry expanding to the upper reaches of the Delaware Valley in 1722 and the Susquehanna watershed in 1737. Cornwall Furnace was built in 1742 in what would become Lebanon County, and ironmaking crossed the Susquehanna in 1750 with a forge at Boiling Springs in Cumberland County.[17]

Three or four miners could keep a single furnace supplied by loosening and breaking up the ore that was then transported to the surface. Limestone could be quarried in a similar fashion. However, the production of charcoal was a complicated, labor-intensive, and time-consuming task that had major consequences for the natural world. Indeed, Britons feared a wood shortage on their mainland in the sixteenth and seventeenth centuries that was caused in part by ironmaking, and in 1664, John Evelyn, a British arborist, suggested that the burgeoning empire center its industry in the colonies to attempt to conserve its forests. "Twere better to purchase all our Iron out of America," he concluded, "than to exhaust our woods at home." Each day a typical iron smelting furnace consumed charcoal amounting to an acre of forest, meaning that the furnaces needed an enormous supply of wood, resulting in extensive forest clearing. Since it was more cost-efficient to ship finished products than tons of bulky wood, colonial iron furnaces were generally located in the rural hinterland. Skilled workers carefully constructed mounds of logs, generally black oak, snuggly capped with soil and leaves that would prevent much air from entering the burn piles. Low oxygen fostered high heat without flame that drove water and soluble minerals from wood, leaving nearly pure carbon. When the worker in charge of the process, called a collier, judged it complete, the fire was extinguished by cutting off all oxygen.[18]

At the iron furnace itself, workers brought ingredients to the top of a hollow pyramid-shaped stack, beginning with charcoal that was allowed to burn down until nothing remained but glowing coals. Then workers poured in alternating layers of charcoal, iron ore, and limestone at regular intervals, day and night. Iron liquefied at 2,700 degrees Fahrenheit and would trickle downward through the specially shaped furnace. Less heavy limestone would bind to impurities in the ore to form a liquid slag that also dropped through the furnace but floated on top of the liquid iron. Waterwheels fed a steady supply of compressed air that bubbled up through the melting raw materials, increasing the heat and hastening separation of iron from the ore. After about twelve hours, workers would unplug a hole near the bottom, allowing slag to drain away, which was carried off and thrown on an ever growing slag heap. Opening the lowest hole then allowed the molten iron to flow into long channels formed in the sand floor of a casting house, with shorter channels extending from them at right angles called "pigs" (because they resembled suckling piglets) or into direct cast molds to make hollowware, skillets, kettles, ornate stove plates, and other items. The pig iron bars then went to a refinery forge, where they would be reheated and made into wrought iron by mechanically hammering out remaining impurities before being sent to a variety of finishing mills on-site or into the marketplace for use by blacksmiths.[19]

The backcountry of Pennsylvania was far removed from the wealthy plantations of the Caribbean and the silver and gold mines of Spanish America, but it is important to keep in mind that the mastery of the natural world necessary to transform raw resources into refined sugar, gold ingots, or finished iron went hand in hand with the mastery over fellow human beings, whether enslaved people, indentured servants, or wage workers. On the eve of the American Revolution, the colonial iron industry in British North America produced one-seventh of the world's estimated output and was growing steadily, with Pennsylvania leading all the colonies with more than seventy forges and furnaces. As Beverly Tomek notes in *Slavery and Abolition in Pennsylvania*, "Slavery grew out of white aversion to doing hard work for someone else's profit," and iron forges formed the largest industrial use of enslaved labor in the colony. Even if Pennsylvania was dubbed the "best poor man's country" by one scholar, its working landscapes largely reserved for White men the profits derived from nature's bounty. You can see an example of this by visiting a small park near Cornwall named for Governor Dick, an enslaved African man purchased by the iron master Peter Grubb in 1776 just as his furnace began producing the cannon and shot needed for the Continental Army in the Revolutionary War.[20]

A "Greene Country Towne"

"The wisdom of Lycurgus and Solon never conferred on man one half of the blessings and uninterrupted prosperity which the Pennsylvanians now possess . . . : either nature or the climate seems to be more favourable here to the arts and sciences, than to any other American province." This is how Crèvecoeur began his description of a visit in the late 1760s to the farm of John Bartram, "the first botanist, in this new hemisphere," along the Schuylkill River just outside of Philadelphia. "It is to this simple man that America is indebted for several useful discoveries, and the knowledge of many new plants," Crèvecoeur continued. "I had been greatly prepossessed in his favour by the extensive correspondence which I knew he held with the most eminent Scotch and French botanists." A self-trained man who began his foray into botany by devoting a portion of his farm to growing plants he found interesting, Bartram underscored Philadelphia's role as a key node in the transatlantic marketplace of ideas about nature, as well as its physical products. Bartram cofounded the American Philosophical Society in 1743 along with Benjamin Franklin, who in 1765 successfully lobbied George III to name the gentleman farmer as King's Botanist for North America.[21]

As with the farms and iron furnaces of the countryside, the social world of Philadelphia was carved from the natural world of which it remained a part. Unlike the more haphazard development of the backcountry, however, William Penn provided detailed instructions to his agents that revealed his desire to avoid the congestion of London, which had suffered an outbreak of bubonic plague in 1665 and a disastrous fire the following year. Hoping to establish a community that was both profitable and reflective of heavenly virtue, Penn ordered his surveyor to lay out the new city of Philadelphia as a "greene Country Towne which will never be burnt, and always be wholesome." Colonial officials platted a grid of streets running a mile along the Delaware River from Vine Street to South Street and two miles west to the Schuylkill River, for a total of 1,200 acres. Two wide streets—Market and Broad—divided the city into four sections, with a central ten-acre park and eight-acre common areas in the middle of each quadrant.[22]

Philadelphia served as "nature's entrepôt," where merchants transformed the products of the colony's farms, foundries, and forests into commodities that fueled the Atlantic world. Despite the initial planning efforts, rapid growth created a dense urban place centered on the waterfronts, while the city's common areas became refuse dumps, execution yards, and paupers' gravesites. The Quaker city was closer to the Caribbean than either Boston or New York, so much of the excess wheat produced in nearby Lancaster, Bucks,

and Chester counties was destined to feed enslaved Africans on sugar plantations. In return, Philadelphians received rum, coffee, molasses, and the cur-
rency needed to buy imported goods, including enslaved humans such as
those destined for work at Cornwall Furnace. Urban growth was thus tied
tightly to the success of rural working landscapes, with more than a dozen
shipyards lining the waterfront to build vessels that would be filled with farm
products. Meanwhile, distilleries, tanneries, slaughterhouses, and other unattractive industries clustered along Dock Creek, where their stinking effluent
could be dispersed downstream into the Delaware River. Upstream from the
Schuylkill River, eight water-powered mills lined the fast-flowing Wissahickon
Creek by 1730, keeping the immigrant artisans of Germantown busy processing grain. By 1793, this number had grown to twenty-four. Prudent investments in these and other industries, including the iron foundries stretching
north and west from the city, produced great wealth for those free men, like
Benjamin Franklin, who were able to own property and reap the benefits of
their and others' labor.[23]

The scientific and intellectual ideas that permeated the genteel class of late
eighteenth-century Philadelphia owed their origins to the wealth created by
harnessing the power of nature and controlling humans. When Thomas Paine
visited in 1774, he commented, "Almost every Philadelphian . . . has some
scientific interest or business." One French visitor in the 1780s explained, "[in
this] most beautiful [city] you will find more well-educated men, more knowledge of politics, and literature, and more political and learned societies than
anywhere else in the United States." The city's reputation came, at least in
part, from the activities of Franklin, its most famous citizen, who, having established his fortune early as a newspaper printer, turned his attention to
politics, civic improvement, and scientific discovery, each of which had significant bearing on the city's and state's environmental history. As a politician
and diplomat, Franklin aligned himself with the political faction opposed to
the power of the Penn family (the "anti-proprietary party") and worked to
foster unity among the British North American colonies and ease tensions
with Native Americans, even as colonists rapidly pushed into the continental
interior. As a scientist and engineer, Franklin made improvements to stoves,
chimneys, and lamps that increased efficiency, and his study of ocean currents
helped to reduce travel times across the Atlantic.[24]

It was his attention to civic improvement, particularly in opposing water
pollution, that later earned Franklin the moniker "America's first environmentalist." In 1739 he and his neighbors (unsuccessfully) petitioned the colonial government to remove the tanneries and slaughterhouses along Dock
Creek and the Delaware River near his printshop on Market Street (Figure

Figure 1.3 The landing of Penn at Dock Creek, Philadelphia, ca. 1830. (Credit: Gift of Mr. And Mrs. Meyer P. Potamkin, The State Museum of Pennsylvania.)

1.3). He wrote in his *Pennsylvania Gazette* that the creek was choked with all manner of offal and that the fish "soon floated belly up." During the 1760s, he led a Philadelphia committee to regulate water pollution in the city between the Schuylkill and Delaware rivers. While he spent much of his later life pursuing diplomatic activities for the young nation that carried him far from Philadelphia, the city and its environment were never far from his mind. Months before his death in 1790, he added a codicil to his will bequeathing funds to the city for long-term improvements to its water system.[25]

Franklin's Philadelphia was a center of the transatlantic trade in ideas due to its relatively democratic society of expanding wealth and population and an openness to questioning received wisdom among its Quaker founders. Other leading figures combined political aspirations with an attention to the natural world, such as Benjamin Rush, a signer of the Declaration of Independence and medical doctor who focused on the human body and theories of disease, and Charles Wilson Peale, a painter and naturalist whose personal museum collection developed into the Pennsylvania Academy of Fine Arts. The genteel homes lining the banks of the Schuylkill and Delaware rivers showcased the highest architectural standards available in the colonies, and their gardens were the place where the socially prominent, as well as intellectuals and artists, gathered to exchange ideas. Beginning in the 1730s, John Bartram traveled throughout the Mid-Atlantic region collecting specimens from the heights of the Appalachian Mountains to lowland swamps and coastal estuaries. He and his descendants developed a thriving and well-respected nursery along the Schuylkill, with boxes of seeds and seedlings shipped to some of the finest colonial and European gardens of the age. For some, cultivating North American plants was a sign of refinement and cosmopolitan taste. For others, the quest was about empire building more directly as royal botanists such as the Frenchman André Michaux were tasked with finding practical knowledge about American flora that might benefit merchants and royal navies. Indeed, as learning spaces, botanical gardens functioned much like the surgical theaters of the time: built environments that manifested the scientific authority of the host.[26]

This Enlightenment fascination with ordering the natural world developed in tandem with revolutionary ideas about "natural law." Under the influence of John Locke, Philadelphia thinkers such as Franklin and Rush increasingly questioned the divine authority of monarchs in much the same way they questioned inherited wisdom about the natural world. Of the first 375 books that Franklin and his cohort gathered for North America's first circulating library, more were by Locke than any other author. Central to Locke's ideas about natural law was the notion that by farming, mining, logging, and other activities, humans effectively joined their labor to the environment and made that modified nature their property. This vision of the world appealed to colonists who saw themselves as having arrived in a primeval state of wilderness and, by their efforts, transformed it into civilization. Locke pointed to the British colonies as an example of how humanity created property and society from the Earth's raw resources. "Thus in the beginning," he had written, "all the World was America." In *Letters from a Farmer in Pennsylvania*, written in response to the Townshend Acts beginning in 1767, John Dickinson, an important figure in Pennsylvania politics, a member of the Continental Congress, and later a delegate to the Constitutional Convention, supported his argument that Parliament had no right to tax the colonies with appeals to natural law. "We cannot be happy without being free," Dickinson wrote. "We cannot be free without being secure in our own property. . . . We cannot be secure in our property, if, without our consent, others may take it away." Of course, this ignored both the activities of Native Americans and their rights to the working landscapes they inhabited.[27]

Nature of Revolution

"The shot heard round the world" that launched the American Revolution may have been fired in Lexington, Massachusetts, but the global conflict that set the stage for that war began in Pennsylvania with George Washington's ill-fated expedition to counter the French at the Forks of the Ohio in 1754. As Washington and his men slowly hacked their way through vast forests and later fought a last-ditch effort to stave off defeat at Fort Necessity, the young militia officer was motivated not only by the claim of the British Empire to the territory west of the Appalachian Mountains but also by the need to assert the title of the Virginia colony to an area it was contesting with its northern neighbor. Indeed, for the rest of his life, even as he pursued his broader imperial and later revolutionary goals, the trained surveyor was always on the lookout for choice properties that could be turned into profitable investments. "Any person who neglects hunting out good lands, and in some measure marking and distinguishing them for his own, in order to keep others from settling them will never regain it," Washington wrote to the Pennsylvania surveyor William Crawford, with whom he set out on a survey expedition in 1770 from Fort Pitt to identify bounty lands owed to his fellow veterans of the Seven Years' War.[28]

The Seven Years' War had every bit as profound an impact on Pennsylvania's working landscapes as it did on its politics and culture. By the war's outbreak, the colony had become the breadbasket of the British Empire, and a steady stream of wagons filled with corn, wheat, and hay, some arranged by Franklin himself, provided the logistical fodder that made victory possible. The introduction of direct cash payments during the war and completion of the Braddock and Forbes roads drew backcountry farmers more directly into the broader transatlantic marketplace, while the removal of the French fueled even more intense land speculation by wealthy investors and unauthorized occupation by newer immigrants. However, the violence of the 1750s and 1760s ended the relatively peaceful relations between Native Americans and Europeans in Pennsylvania, with the latter increasingly viewing the former as the "merciless Indian Savages" later depicted in the Declaration of Independence. The attempt by King George III to impose a more orderly process of land acquisition, embodied in the Royal Proclamation of 1763, had the opposite effect as an estimated fifty thousand settlers crossed the Appalachians over the next decade into a landscape largely beyond the reach of government authority.[29]

Both Enlightenment ideas about nature and tensions over who should control the physical lands beyond the Appalachians were at the forefront as representatives from throughout the colonies gathered in Philadelphia in 1775 to debate the founding of a new nation. Like George Washington, Thomas Jefferson and many other members of the Continental Congress had joined the speculative frenzy of the previous decades that had been thrown into doubt by the king's "raising the conditions of new Appropriations of Lands," as their declaration described the Proclamation of 1763. In addition to being the capital of the new United States, Philadelphia was the gathering point for the agricultural and mineral riches of the surrounding countryside. Pennsylvania iron foundries provided cannon and ammunition, while farms provided livestock and grain.[30]

Following Washington's disastrous evacuation of New York City in the fall of 1776, what was left of his army retreated to Philadelphia without having won a single significant engagement. Their fortunes began to change with the famous Christmas crossing of the Delaware River, after which 2,400 Americans defeated 1,500 Hessian mercenaries stationed in Trenton. Weather played a pivotal role in the lead-up to the battle, as the already exhausted Americans reached the river just as a howling nor'easter "blew a perfect hurricane," in the words of one soldier. The same storm that made the river crossing such a challenge, however, also helped shield the army's advance, allowing it to surprise the enemy the next day. A few months later, in the spring of 1777, British General William Howe launched a two-pronged attack to divide the colonies and capture Philadelphia. The physical environment played a key role in this campaign, as well, at times helping and at other times harming the revolutionary cause. In September, for example, a massive downpour soaked the ammunition of the Continentals, protected only by single-flap cartridge boxes hastily made of unseasoned leather. The resulting loss of an estimated 400,000 rounds of ammunition in what became known as the "Battle of the Clouds" left Washington's army scrambling to acquire more gunpowder and unable to engage with the enemy. When the flooding Schuylkill River finally receded, the way was clear for the British to take Philadelphia without a shot fired.[31]

With transatlantic supply lines stretched thin, controlling the products of Pennsylvania's working landscapes was essential to both the British and the Continental armies for supporting their war efforts. As with the Seven Years' War, victory depended to a significant extent on who could best feed hungry bellies and ensure the general health of both men and their mounts. Even as the drills of the Prussian-born officer Friedrich von Steuben helped establish military discipline in the winter camp at Valley Forge, the cold, poorly clothed soldiers of the Continental Army faced starvation, as well as diseases such as typhus, dysentery, and influenza. Washington combated the latter with strict sanitation orders and an inoculation campaign to protect against smallpox, but by January 1778 the army's quartermaster and commissary departments had collapsed. At the same time, spies reported that General Howe, who was

Figure 1.4 The American troops at Valley Forge. (From: Benson Lossing, *Our Country: A Household History for All Readers* [New York: Henry J. Johnson, 1879].)

dealing with his own supply problems, was about to launch a "grand Forage" of the surrounding countryside. Desperate to provide for his men and determined to prevent food and forage from falling into enemy hands, on February 12 Washington ordered Major-General Nathanael Greene to "carry of & secure all such Horses as are suitable for Cavalry or for Draft and all Cattle & Sheep fit for Slaughter together with every kind of Forage" that could be found within twenty miles west of the Delaware River. Anything that could not be carried off Greene was to "immediately Cause to be destroyed." Over the next six weeks, Greene and his subordinates, include General Anthony Wayne, foraged as far as New Jersey (Figure 1.4).[32]

Following the entry of the French into the war and the retreat of the British Army to New York City in June 1778, the focus of the war shifted from Pennsylvania. However, long-standing tensions between and among various Euro-American and Native American factions boiled over into what amounted to "an American civil war" in the Susquehanna Valley and Appalachian Mountains; in the words of the historian Colin Calloway, "Whites killed Indians, Indians killed whites, Indians killed Indians, and whites killed whites in guerilla [*sic*] warfare that was localized, vicious, and tolerated no neutrals." Just as in nonindigenous communities, Native peoples served on both sides of the conflict, as individuals and in groups, while many others simply tried to get on with their lives the best they could.[33]

Scholars have described the process by which, as in British North America, an immigrant population seeks to fully displace and replace an existing population as "settler colonialism." Perhaps the most striking example of European colonists mobilizing environmental destruction to further their goals during the American Revolution took place in the Wyoming Valley along the northeastern border with New York. Despite the adoption of commercial hunting, as well as the fruit, potatoes, pigs, chickens, cattle, and other foodstuffs introduced by Europeans, many Native Americans remained largely dependent on the "three sisters" of corn, beans, and squash. As a result, even a relatively small force could decimate entire communities by destroying their working landscapes. On May 31, 1779, George Washington ordered General John Sullivan "to carry the war into the Heart of the Country of the [Haudenosaunee] six nations; to cut off their settlements, destroy their next Year's crops, and do them every other mischief of which time and circumstances will permit." Washington concluded, "It will be essential to ruin their crops now in the ground and prevent them planting more."[34]

Sullivan's expedition broke the last bastion of Native American power in the state and eventually led to the 1784 Treaty of Fort Stanwix that ceded Haudenosaunee claims to much of their territory. By the end of October, American forces had burned more than forty villages and, with their food stores destroyed, drove five thousand starving Haudenosaunee to Fort Niagara seeking British protection during what was one of the coldest winters on record. Of course, many individuals of indigenous ancestry quietly continued their lives by blending into Euro-American communities, but aside from a small plot of land along the Allegheny River granted to the Dutch Seneca war chief Cornplanter by the new federal government, no recognized Native American community remained by the year 1800 in Pennsylvania.

––––––––––

By the end of the American Revolution, the more communal understanding of land use practiced by the first Pennsylvanians was almost fully replaced with a vision of private land ownership as the basis for individual wealth and the foundation of Jefferson's new "empire of liberty." However, the darker side of Enlightenment efforts to apply rational order over unruly environments and "natural law" on the citizens of a new nation meant that both were often based on unfree labor, whether those workers were enslaved Pennsylvanians of African descent toiling on iron plantations or impoverished tenant farmers giving up a portion of their crop to large landowners. Concessions by Virginia, Connecticut, Massachusetts, and New York established the state's modern boundaries by 1790, while rapid population growth increasingly drove settlement and resource extraction west to the Ohio River Valley and north to the far reaches of the Susquehanna watershed. Finally, while Philadelphia lost its status as the preeminent American city in the early decades of the nineteenth century, it continued to serve as nature's entrepôt, gathering the vast material resources of the state's interior and shaping ideas about the natural world through culture and politics.

2

WORKING LANDSCAPES

I N SPRING OF 1842, the English novelist Charles Dickens left Harrisburg by canalboat—"a barge with a little house in it," according to his description—powered by three horses attached to a towrope. "The boy upon the leader smacked his whip, the rudder creaked and groaned complainingly, and we had begun our journey." Along the way, Dickens lamented, "The eye was pained to see the stumps of great trees thickly strewn in every field of wheat . . . where settlers had been burning down the trees, and where their wounded bodies lay about, like those of murdered creatures." After a few days, "We arrived at the foot of the mountain, which is crossed by railroad"—ten inclined planes that allowed canalboats to summit the Allegheny Front. "Occasionally the rails are laid upon the extreme verge of a giddy precipice," he explained, "and looking from the carriage window, the traveller gazes sheer down, without a stone or scrap of fence between, into the mountain depths below."[1]

Nineteenth-century industrial expansion transformed Pennsylvania as new canals and then railroads connected hungry markets with far-off sources of food, fiber, and finished products. Farmers increasingly mechanized, and the need to serve distant populations prompted important shifts in agricultural working landscapes. Urban environments, too, underwent dramatic changes as swelling population and industrial growth exacerbated pollution and disease outbreaks. Philadelphia was an early leader in creating public water systems and parks, but the experiences of residents living in smoky Pittsburgh and myriad market towns and mining camps were equally important in understanding how nonhuman nature shaped the state's urban history. Finally, timber, coal, steel, and railroads undergirded growth of heavy industry, with dramatic impacts that extended from fetid rivers to clear-cut mountainsides and smoky skies. However, as Dickens's revulsion at the dead trees along his route suggests, the cultural seeds for the conservation movement were already being planted.

Artificial Rivers and Iron Horses

Just a decade earlier, Dickens's journey would have taken nearly a month, but the completion of Pennsylvania's Main Line of Public Works in 1834 reduced this time to such an extent that, having left Harrisburg on Friday, by Monday evening "furnace fires and clanking hammers on the banks of the canal, warned us that we approached the termination of this part of our journey . . . and were at Pittsburg." Transportation was key to transforming natural resources into marketable commodities. Earlier trail systems were often unpassable by wagons, so merchants and farmers continued to use packhorse trains through the mid-nineteenth century, especially in the central and western parts of the state. Nevertheless, between 1750 and 1812, a combination of public and private funders improved several roadways, especially between Philadelphia and the Susquehanna River, including the Philadelphia–Lancaster Turnpike in 1795. This later became the eastern link in the Pennsylvania Road through Harrisburg, Carlisle, Shippensburg, Bedford, Ligonier, and on to Pittsburgh, which was paved with stone by 1820. Nevertheless, most roads remained largely seasonal in nature as spring rains and winter snow often made travel through the Appalachians virtually impossible for months each year. Maintenance was left to local landowners or paid for by a system of tolls that further increased travel costs.[2]

Commercial life thus largely remained either a local or an aquatic affair, with overland travel generally an expensive and time-consuming option. Indeed, it cost more to haul coal eighty miles from the new anthracite fields of northeastern Pennsylvania's Wyoming Valley to Philadelphia than to ship it three thousand miles from Britain. The farther inland that settlements reached, the less likely they could depend on the vagaries of rivers that required fighting a current when moving upstream and could flood in the spring, be reduced to a trickle in late summer, and freeze in the winter. Consequently, as early as 1762 Philadelphia merchants petitioned the Provincial Assembly to explore the Susquehanna River's west branch for a potential connection to the Ohio River, and Benjamin Franklin's American Philosophical Society recommended a canal linking the Schuylkill and Susquehanna rivers in 1771.[3]

Figure 2.1 Schuylkill canalboats being built for the Philadelphia and Reading Railroad Company, Highspire, Pennsylvania, ca. 1870s. (Courtesy: Pennsylvania State Archives, Photograph Collection, MG-218.)

Political infighting, competition between Philadelphia and Baltimore for the Susquehanna River trade, and fiscal conservatism prevented the construction of all but a few local canals until the completion of the Erie Canal in 1825 threatened the permanent economic displacement of Philadelphia by New York City. Unlike in New York, where the Mohawk and Hudson rivers provided the only natural break in the Appalachian Mountains north of Alabama, canal builders in Pennsylvania faced the daunting task of overcoming thousands of feet of elevation change. By the time the "Main Line," as it was known, connected Philadelphia to Pittsburgh and the Ohio River in 1840, it required 726 miles of waterways and other infrastructure, including a thirty-mile stretch of railroads and ten inclined planes to carry traffic over the steep rise of the Allegheny Front (Figure 2.1).[4]

Even when it was finally completed, Pennsylvania's trans-Appalachian transportation system was no match for the cheaper and faster Erie Canal. Faced with cost overruns and the never-ending need for subsidies, the General Assembly abandoned plans for a canal linking the Main Line to Philadelphia and instead chartered a new railroad to carry passengers and freight to the town of Columbia on the Susquehanna River. The Philadelphia and Columbia Railroad began operation in 1832 as rapid improvements in steam power fueled a decisive shift toward railroads. Originally employing teams of horses, the line quickly shifted to locomotives, including the *George Washington*, which in 1836 pulled a loaded train up the Belmont plane at the eastern end of the line, demonstrating that locomotives could surmount substantial grades. The railroad era had begun.

Steam power revolutionized transportation and transformed Pennsylvania's working landscapes. In addition to the Philadelphia and Columbia, local investors launched the Cumberland Valley Railroad between Harrisburg and Chambersburg in 1837. The next year, the Philadelphia, Wilmington, and Baltimore Railroad began service, as did a route between Baltimore and York, and in 1843 the Philadelphia and Reading Railroad began shipping anthracite coal directly to the city. Finally, in 1846 the legislature granted a charter for a railroad to connect Harrisburg and Pittsburgh to compete with Maryland's Baltimore and Ohio Railroad (B&O), which was rapidly progressing toward the Ohio River. By 1882, the Pennsylvania Railroad had become the largest corporation in the world, with a budget second in the nation only to that of the U.S. government.[5]

Canals and railroads integrated local environments within broader regional networks. Early entrepreneurs used water to power gristmills and redirected streams into industrial canals to provide more regular sources of energy as communities grew. By the 1820s, entirely new towns emerged at key junctions, near lockhouses, and alongside the large reservoirs needed to keep channels at a consistent depth. Canals crossed valleys, turnpikes, and waterways, requiring spans that ranged from modest culverts to enormous aqueducts over the larger rivers. Facing a dearth of skilled workers and quarries necessary for masonry arch structures common in Europe, Pennsylvania's canal builders turned to abundant forests in developing a new type of wooden truss bridge named for Thomas Burr, who used his patented design in a series of very long timber-frame arch bridges across the Susquehanna and elsewhere. Of course, this resulted in the harvesting of enormous amounts of wood along the canal routes, and since wood deteriorated much faster than stone, it meant that infrastructure was in constant need of repair.[6]

Hollidaysburg, along the Juniata River in what is now Blair County, illustrates the effects canal building had on working landscapes. The town had been settled in the late eighteenth century along a path through the Appalachian Mountains, but its rugged remoteness meant that it still had a population of only about seventy-five as late as 1827. Engineers selected the site as the transfer point from the Main Line's Juniata Division to the Portage Railroad that would carry passengers and freight over the Allegheny Front. Five years later, the town had ballooned to three thousand residents and was dominated by a gigantic artificial pool, built by hand, that was six feet deep, 120 feet wide, and two miles long where three branches of the Juniata River converged. At the height of the canal era, the docks of this new inland port serviced a boat every twenty minutes, with large warehouses built to handle freight and hotels and taverns springing up to cater to boatmen and travelers.[7]

Hollidaysburg "has the air of a new clearing, and looks so unfinished, that one might suppose it to have been built within a year," declared one traveler in 1835. "Its site is good, rising gradually from the basin to a pleasant elevation. Many substantial buildings are going up, and it is evident that rapid increase is the destiny of the town." In addition to passenger traffic, the canal carried everything from pianos to flour, cement, and nails, supplanting local sources for consumer goods while connecting local producers to distant markets. Entrepreneurs built iron foundries and machine shops to fabricate implements and tools from pig iron produced in nearby charcoal furnaces, such as Allegheny Furnace in what is now downtown Altoona. While most of these early ventures eventually faded as new technologies emerged and the center of the iron industry shifted to other areas, the McLanahan Corporation, founded in 1835, has continued to operate for six generations to the present day.[8]

Canals were artificial constructs, but they remained intimately tied to the natural processes of rivers. Engineers struggled to keep sufficient water levels in summer, and in winter canals were blocked by ice, while spring and fall flooding could damage locks, bridges, and other infrastructure. Railroads, by contrast, could run year-round and, once the technological challenge of building sufficiently powerful steam engines was overcome, could go places canals simply could not. However, this required a much more sophisticated command-and-control structure and supply chains. Massive quantities of wood were needed for ties, bridges, and other infrastructure, not to mention as fuel for hungry boilers. Indeed, timber harvesting and the growth of railroads went together as expanding deforestation required opening increasingly distant mountain valleys in the state's north and west. Steam engines also required a constant and accessible supply of water, which engineers provided via trackside water tanks that drew from holding reservoirs constructed at higher elevations. Finally, as companies gradually shifted from wood to coal for fuel, extensive new mining operations resulted in the pollution of local streams and, especially in the case of bituminous coal, massive increases in air pollution.

If Hollidaysburg represents the iconic canal community, then Altoona, its neighbor five miles to the north, aptly illustrates the working landscapes of the railroad age. To avoid the operating problems of the steep Allegheny Portage, Pennsylvania Railroad engineers plotted an alternative route to climb the Allegheny Front from the Juniata River. At the crucial location where the grade increased significantly, executives founded a company town centered on extensive railyards and repair shops that was near iron ore deposits, as well as coal, timber, and other resources. In 1850, the railroad completed a single track to Altoona, and in December the first train ran to Pittsburgh using portions of the Portage Railroad, a temporary solution that lasted until the completion of the famous Horseshoe Curve in 1854. As new repair and fabricating shops opened for railcars, bridges, and tracks, Altoona grew rapidly from a few settlers in 1850 to 3,591 in 1860 and more than ten thousand in 1870. This new urban industrial landscape repeated itself in communities throughout the state, where time was no longer measured by the sun or passing seasons but by the steam whistle's scream and measured cadence of the conductor's pocket watch.[9]

This new industrial geography also changed Pennsylvania farms, especially in those southeastern and south-central areas close to urban centers. Prior to 1830, the state's agricultural landscapes remained "rather jumbled and inconsistent," in the words of the historian Sally McMurry, with a recently settled interior of "small log houses, crude outbuildings and tiny clearings," in contrast to the southeast, where "new domestic markets and pest problems had forced a transition to an integrated grain and livestock economy." In long-established areas of Chester, Berks, and Bucks counties, dairying grew rapidly, with butter and fluid milk becoming more important. Even as railroads displaced horses and wagons (or canalboats) for long-distance hauling, the shift to coal and steam engines created demand for horses in agricultural, industrial, and urban settings, with the result that hay became an important cash crop. Grain, tobacco, and dairy flourished in Lancaster County, while Adams and York counties developed one of the nation's early fruit belts with the advent of industrial canning. By 1850, competition from grain growers in midwestern states pushed many families to focus on providing fruits and vegetables, poultry, beef, and pork for urban customers through regional markets and truck farming.[10]

The effect of the transportation revolution on agricultural working landscapes is particularly evident in the Cumberland Valley. The 1835 report of the Cumberland Valley Railroad's chief engineer emphasized that "nearly the whole of the Rail Road will pass through a finely cultivated country, abounding with some of the richest limestone farms in the State." "When it is considered," he continued, that in addition to waterpower for mills and "iron ore of the very best quality and in great abundance," "a large majority of the farms are yet too extensive, easily admitting of a more minute division, and consequent increase of products, some idea may be formed of the extent of the business" that the line could generate. Average farm size in the state did drop steadily even as production greatly increased while generally remaining quite diversified, especially by today's standards. Barn styles, outbuildings, and even farmhouses reflected these changes, as the Pennsylvania forebay barn, with its emphasis on versatility and ability to accommodate both grain and livestock production, became the overwhelming choice for farmers. The Diller barn in Cumberland County, for example, was originally built in 1807 but was expanded in the mid-nineteenth century to accommodate five threshing floors, two hay mows, and a seven-bin granary, reflecting the higher-intensity production of the owner's nearly five hundred acre farm.[11]

Building Urban Environments

Ten years before Dickens's trip to Pittsburgh on the Main Line, another famous English writer offered her impressions of the Pennsylvania landscape. Largely unimpressed with Philadelphia, Frances Trollope did find "one spot, however, about a mile from the town, which presents a lovely scene." She explained: "At a most beautiful point of the Schuylkill River, the water has been forced up into a magnificent reservoir, ample and elevated enough to send it through the whole city. The vast yet simple machinery by which this is achieved is open to the public, who resort in such numbers to see it, that several evening stages run from Philadelphia to Fair Mount for their accommodation." Several smaller communities created public water systems during the colonial era, including Bethlehem in 1755, but Philadelphia's development in 1800 of a steam-powered waterworks designed by Benjamin Latrobe was the first public water supply of any major American city. It was replaced by the larger water-powered Fairmount Water Works (Figure 2.2) that was admired by Trollope and, later, Dickens himself as "no less ornamental than useful," with the whole city supplied at a "trifling expense."[12]

Even as the revolution in transportation transformed the rural environment, Pennsylvania's towns and cities exploded in population. Between 1800 and 1850, greater Philadelphia grew from 68,000 to more than 350,000 residents and then to 566,000 by 1860, making it the second largest U.S. city and the fourth largest city in the Atlantic world (after London, Paris, and New York). Similarly, Allegheny County (Pittsburgh) grew from about 15,000 in 1800 to 138,000 by 1850 and more than 180,000 by 1860. With Philadelphia's dominance in foreign trade eclipsed by New York City, the city looked to its hinterland and the west for opportunities, which drove investment by merchants within the city and throughout the state in turnpikes, canals, and, later, railroads. At the beginning of the eighteenth century, Philadelphia was the nation's largest producer of hand-crafted goods, but as transportation improvements and overall population growth expanded the marketplace, entre-

Figure 2.2 Fairmount Water Works, half of a stereo view, ca. 1860. (Courtesy: Library Company of Philadelphia.)

preneurs increasingly substituted water-powered machines for skilled artisans to increase volume and lower costs. The city's proximity to the cotton-growing South meant that Philadelphia merchants developed a symbiotic relationship with slave-controlling planters, who provided raw material that was processed in a growing number of textile mills. By 1800 there were eight mills along the Wissahickon Creek in the nearby village of Roxborough, and the completion of a short industrial canal along the Schuylkill River provided sites for more mills in the 1820s.[13]

Rivers were equally important to the development of Pittsburgh, though the stream gradient of the Allegheny Plateau was not as conducive to water-powered mills as it was along the Atlantic Seaboard Fall Line. Instead, rivers served as transportation corridors, and their banks provided some of the only flat land available for development amid the jumbled terrain. Pittsburgh and its neighboring communities across the Ohio, Allegheny, and Monongahela rivers spread along the valleys and only gradually worked their way up steep escarpments. Especially before the completion of the Main Line system in the 1820s, the city's economy was oriented not toward Philadelphia, but downstream toward the growing communities of the Ohio and Mississippi valleys. Entrepreneurs fashioned the region's clay into pottery and bricks; used local sand in making glass; and milled the iron from rural blast furnaces into finished products. Easily accessible and abundant bituminous coal fueled it all and created the city's notoriously smoky skies; as early as 1821, one observer was declaring that Pittsburgh could be called the "Birmingham of America."[14]

The general pattern of community development beginning along rivers and, later, turnpikes and eventually canals also held true for Pennsylvania's smaller communities. By 1840, in growing villages such as Allentown (pop. 2,493) on the Lehigh River, Wilkes-Barre (pop. 1,718) on the Susquehanna River, and Warren (pop. 737) on the Allegheny River, as well as Erie (pop. 3,412) on Lake Erie, prosperous merchants, lawyers, and artisans established a pattern of locating their shops in the center of town "convenient to the pulse of commerce and industry," as one historian put it, with affluent citizens living in spacious houses on wide avenues and the less well-off crowding into smaller residences on side streets. The lack of public transportation meant that all communities remained compact, with owners and laborers living within walking distance of their work and thus, generally, within the oftentimes narrow flatlands along river and creek banks. The death of more than two thousand people in the infamous Johnstown Flood of 1889 can be traced partly to this development pattern, which placed the commercial and residential heart of the city of Johnstown within the narrow confines of the Conemaugh River Valley (Figure 2.3). That flood, caused by the failure of the South Fork Dam, which was originally built as a reservoir for the Main Line, was exacerbated by decades of deforestation that magnified the effects of heavy rain on the inadequately maintained dam.[15]

Fierce political and commercial battles took place over which groups of entrepreneurs and speculators would control access to the state's timber, iron, and coal resources. In Milford along the Delaware River, for example, Constantine Pinchot, a wealthy Frenchman exiled for his support of Napoleon, arrived with his family in 1820 and purchased four hundred acres of farmland that he leased out to other new immigrants. Trading the farm's produce, as well as local lumber and grain, for finished goods from New York City and Philadelphia, Pinchot and later his son Cyrille used the profits to buy more

Figure 2.3 Cambria Iron Company, Gautier Works, Johnstown, Pennsylvania, ca. 1968.
(Courtesy: Library of Congress, Prints and Photographs Division.)

timberland in Pennsylvania, New York, Michigan, and Wisconsin, thus solidifying both his family's wealth and the success of his community. An early turnpike connected Milford both to the Erie Canal corridor in New York and Pennsylvania's anthracite region, but in the 1840s the Pennsylvania and Erie Railroad built its line bypassing Milford and leaving the community without an easy connection to the new transportation system. Following a bruising and unsuccessful political battle to secure a spur line, the Pinchots moved the bulk of their business operations to New York City and continued to prosper, while Milford never expanded much beyond the role of country crossroads.[16]

Conversely, Harrisburg, along the Susquehanna River, illustrates the changing urban environment in a growing community. Originally the site of a Susquehannock village where Paxton Creek entered the river, and later a trading fort and ferry, it became the state capital in 1810 because of its central location. While Milford was left behind in the transportation revolution, Theodore Burr finished work in 1817 on his famous wooden "camelback bridge" connecting the two banks of the Susquehanna, and in 1834 the completion of the Main Line placed Harrisburg at the intersection of the state's major east-west and north-south corridors. As in the smaller county seats located along transportation arteries, this combination of political and economic opportunity helped drive population growth in Harrisburg, which reached six thousand residents by the time of Dickens's canal trip in 1842 and more than thirteen thousand residents when it incorporated as a city in 1860. Lumber from the state's vast northern forests, grain, eggs, and produce from the farms of the Cumberland Valley, pig iron from the Juniata Valley, and machine-made textiles from Philadelphia's mills found their way to the warehouses and retail shops on the east bank of the Susquehanna. Nevertheless, as late as 1850, travelers who entered from the south and east by either the canal or the Harrisburg, Portsmouth, Mountjoy and Lancaster Railroad (with cars originally pulled by horses) would have still passed open fields, woodlots, and farmsteads all the way to the city limits.[17]

While Pittsburgh was known for using the lower-grade bituminous coal that created its notoriously smoky skies, Philadelphians throughout the first half of the nineteenth century largely depended on native forests to heat homes and power industry. The city's merchants invested in large swaths of inland forest near iron deposits to create the charcoal necessary for smelting. With the high costs of transportation, most iron foundries remained in these rural sites and shipped finished goods back to Philadelphia. As forests receded, the increasing cost of wood drove innovation in creating furnaces that could use the less smoky and more efficient but hard to start and finicky to maintain anthracite coal. Then, sometime in the fall of 1820, a group of men piloted crude wooden rafts piled with anthracite to a wharf on the eastern side of the city, setting in motion an energy revolution that would transform both rural and urban landscapes.[18]

Over the previous two years, several hundred workers under the direction of the mill owner Josiah White and Erskine Hazard, son of the first U.S. postmaster, had blasted rocks, built dams, and constructed water gates that altered and regulated the flow of the Lehigh River, making regular shipments of anthracite to the city possible. By 1840, the Lehigh Canal had transported nearly 300,000 tons of anthracite to market, fueling the transformation of Philadelphia and other coastal cities. Soon a vast new working landscape emerged in the anthracite region of northeastern Pennsylvania, where eventually one in four acres would be disturbed by mining activity. New immigrants, often poor Irish Catholics, poured into the area to work under extremely difficult circumstances. The completion of the Pennsylvania Railroad between Philadelphia and Pittsburgh in 1852 also provided ample bituminous coal, which was smoky and did not burn as hot as anthracite but was available in even greater quantities. This shift to coal-fired steam power helped launch a new phase of the industrial revolution in America.[19]

As the nineteenth century progressed, the enormous growth prompted by transportation improvements and industrial change put strains on the traditional walking city. The spread of mills and factories along rivers spurred the development of horse-powered omnibuses (adapted from earlier coaches) and then streetcars pulled along rails. This allowed residents to live at greater distances from workplaces that were spreading to areas of cheaper land on the urban outskirts with available waterpower and railroad access. While city neighborhoods remained largely an indiscriminate mix of workshops, homes, stores, stables, and factories, specialized districts began to emerge in the 1840s. A rail line along Market Street and proximity to the port meant that wholesaling and light manufacturing in Philadelphia concentrated east of Seventh Street, where a quarter of the city's workers made goods, such as sails, cigars, boxes, and clothing, that required little or no machinery. Conversely, the first of what would later be called commuter suburbs began to emerge away from the din and clatter of the central city. Even by the early 1850s, for example, Pittsburgh newspapers had begun featuring advertisements for "country residences" where those wealthy enough to afford daily trips on the omnibus lines could avoid the "pent up and vitiated air of crowded cities" and enjoy a "suburban" lifestyle. Similarly, Philadelphia's wealthiest families built sprawling country estates along the Pennsylvania Railroad's "Main Line" west of the city.[20]

Perhaps surprisingly, the development of steam engines prompted a dramatic rise in the need for horses in both rural and urban settings. Fears of noise, speed, and threat of fire from spewing cinders prompted Philadelphia officials to prohibit locomotives within the city. Consequently, train cars had to be unhooked and towed into town by horses. Further, as railroads proliferated throughout the states, companies built their own stations, with little emphasis on interconnection. As a result, horses were needed whenever passengers or goods needed to be transferred from one line to another. Finally, until the advent of electrification in the 1880s, horse-drawn streetcars were the primary means of intra-urban passenger travel. "The whole operation becomes so mechanical," Alexander Easton, an advocate of streetcar adoption noted, "that the horses, when accustomed to the signals of the bell, stop and start without any action on the part of the driver, by which means a timetable can be effectively used." In 1872, fire insurance maps for Philadelphia showed stables located in every neighborhood, and by 1900, when urban equine populations were at their peak, the city was home to more than fifty thousand horses. In turn, this demand for horsepower required the transportation of vast quantities of hay and oats into urban centers and of enormous amounts of manure back into the countryside.[21]

The growth of Pennsylvania cities exacerbated the risk for communicable disease outbreaks. A typical city street in the mid-nineteenth century remained a mixture of mud, straw, and manure to which residents added the contents of chamber pots, food scraps, and other waste. Rain and spring thaws turned these into muddy tracks with deep ruts from wagons. Behind homes, privy vaults lay near wells into which they leaked their contents. Following a yellow fever epidemic in 1793, a young British engineer living in Philadelphia named Benjamin Henry Latrobe proposed a scheme to use steam-powered pumps to lift the water from the Schuylkill River to higher-elevation tanks and distribute it through wooden pipes. At the time there were still only a few steam pumps in the country, but with the leadership of merchants and city officials, the first public water system in a major U.S. city began operation in 1801. Individual homes could connect to the system for $5 a year, or residents could obtain water for free from public hydrants.[22]

Latrobe's initial design quickly proved inadequate, so in 1822 engineers devised a water-powered system with a dam that also created the tranquil "Schuylkill Pool" used for recreation. The industrial nature of the site that lifted water to a reservoir on Fairmount Hill hid behind a Classical Revival exterior that became the tourist attraction described by Trollope and Dickens. In the 1840s, officials also began purchasing upstream properties in what would become Fairmount Park to help protect the water supply from pollution. This massive public investment paid great dividends in 1832 when cholera, the most dangerous gastrointestinal disease to affect humans, spread from India to the Americas. The death rate in Philadelphia was only a quarter that of New York City, which then lacked any good supply of clean water. Pittsburgh, too, completed a waterworks in 1828 using a steam pump to raise water from the Allegheny River to a reservoir on Grant Hill for distribution throughout the city. Smaller communities also worked to develop their public water supplies. For example, in 1825 a private company built a system that pumped water to a reservoir 160 feet above Allentown from which water was distributed through iron pipes. The city then bought the system in 1869 and expanded it. Even after these types of systems were built, however, access to water services remained limited by class, with poor neighborhoods often confined to springs or wells located uncomfortably near privy vaults.[23]

Landscapes of Fire and Smoke

"Near the top of the Chestnut Ridge a promontory looks out over the tops of second-growth saplings to a broad dim country like a cloudy lake washing the lower slopes of the mountain barrier." Muriel Earley Sheppard thus begins *Cloud by Day: The Story of Coal and Coke and People*, painting a literary portrait of an iconic working landscape:

> This is the Coke Region, the land of silver cinders: a strip of undulating valley in southern Pennsylvania, lying between the Allegheny Mountains and the Monongahela River and extending a little beyond, whose mines provide the coal that makes the coke for the great steel mills of Pittsburgh and the Ohio Valley. It is a country of extremes, ugly by day with banks of coke ovens, tipples, sidings, and fields gnawed to the rock with strip-coal operations; luridly beautiful by night when the glare of the ovens paints the sky and works magic with headframes and sooty buildings; a place of great wealth and great poverty, with too much smoke, too much violence, and far too many people.[24]

The massive expansion of heavy industry in the late nineteenth century owes its origins, in part, to the state's enormous lumber resources. Savvy families like the Pinchots created vast fortunes by accumulating land and harvesting trees that could then be applied to other ventures. Timber was always part of the transatlantic economy. Indeed, colonial laws required the best eastern white pine trees near navigable waterways to be marked with "The King's Broad Arrow," three hatchet slashes that reserved them as British Royal Navy masts. Away from the coasts, the vast forests were more often seen as a hindrance, and farmers generally tried to clear their land as quickly as possible, with hand-hewn lumber serving largely local needs for buildings and fences. As communities developed, local entrepreneurs, often farmers, generated extra income by floating logs downstream or building seasonal water-powered mills to serve their neighbors. These sawmills grew in scope as urban expansion drove demand and transportation improvements allowed them to serve distant populations. By the 1840s, thousands of logs were piloted down rivers or hauled on sleds during the winter to regional mills for processing and delivery to customers.[25]

The introduction of steam engines at every stage, from harvesting and processing to distribution and the end products themselves, placed the timber industry at the heart of Pennsylvania's industrial revolution. Lumber companies sent armies of "woodhicks," "bark peelers," and other workers into the vast, formerly inaccessible forests to harvest the white pine, hemlock, and hardwoods necessary to build Pennsylvania's urban centers, as well as new towns and cities that stretched across the Midwest's largely treeless expanses. Besides logs, the tannins in hemlock bark were essential to the chemical processes that transformed cattle skin into supple, seasoned leather belts that distributed energy from steam engines and power canals to machinery. Enormous demand for forest products funded the construction and improvement of railroads, such as the Jersey Shore, Pine Creek, and Buffalo Railway that linked Clearfield County's coalfields north to the New York Central Railroad. "Swampers" built temporary railroad spurs that followed stream banks and switchbacked up mountainsides, allowing powerful locomotives with heavy loads to conquer steep terrain. By the 1880s, steam-powered log loaders had begun to replace one of lumbering's most tedious and backbreaking processes, allowing a crew of three to load railcars with up to one hundred thousand feet of logs each day.[26]

At that rate, industrial logging produced enormous wealth in just a few decades, along with iconic working landscapes. The first, and most impermanent, of these were logging camps: seasonal communities of migrant workers crammed into simple, often portable structures at the end of a temporary spur line. Once logs were felled, limbed, and sorted, workers transported them by river or rail to small towns such as Roulette along the upper reaches of the Allegheny River, where in the mid-1880s local entrepreneurs backed by capital from out-of-state partners established a large window sash and blind factory, a steam mill, and a major tannery. In addition to dozens of rural mill towns like these throughout northern Pennsylvania, more established river communities grew rapidly, especially Williamsport, where local businessmen had created an extensive system of "booms" on the Susquehanna that captured as many as three hundred million board feet at a time. "Boom rats" sorted, made note of ownership, and directed logs to pools outside of thirty-three sawmills that formed the nation's greatest lumber production area. Away from the mills' frenetic energy and danger, Williamsport's industrial elite built enormous mansions along what became known as millionaire's row.[27]

The Susquehanna log boom remained open until 1908, but lumber companies had largely switched to hauling by train decades earlier. Indeed, one the state's first railroads, the Williamsport and Elmira Railroad, opened in 1839 to transport coal and lumber from the northern woods. Beginning in the 1850s, the Philadelphia-based Pennsylvania Railroad set about acquiring these smaller local lines, so that by the Civil War's outbreak it could deliver the state's agricultural and mineral products, along with manufactured goods, to the battlefields of the upper South. The war served as a catalyst that further accelerated the coordination of shipping through a system of trunk lines between the Atlantic coast and the Midwest. Railroad executives served in government positions overseeing wartime distribution, and federal contracts allowed a massive expansion of the Pennsylvania Railroad's capital and infrastructure. With its southern rival, the Baltimore and Ohio, decimated, and the Mississippi River closed to trade for much of the war, the Pennsylvania Railroad was on its way to becoming the world's largest corporation by 1882.[28]

The wartime experiences of one Pennsylvania Railroad executive in particular, Andrew Carnegie, resulted in the application of innovations in corporate administration and financing that revolutionized industrial production, especially of iron and steel. The Pennsylvania Railroad formula for creating economies of scale—"big trains, loaded full, and run fast"—saw Carnegie push inexorably to lower unit costs by producing more goods per investment dollar and cutting labor expenses. His managers used systematic analysis to lower expenditures within manufacturing steps and in the intervals between parts of the overall process through vertical integration. Carnegie Steel's Edgar Thomson Works, located twelve miles south of Pittsburgh along the Monongahela River, demonstrated how this approach to controlling both humans and nature translated into a new type of industrial working landscape. When it opened in 1875, the Edgar Thomson Works featured two five-ton Bessemer converters and a mill capable of producing 225 tons of steel rails daily, which increased dramatically to three thousand tons later in the century. A partnership with the mine owner Henry Clay Frick provided control over high-quality metallurgical coal that was processed into coke, essential for ironmaking, while other Carnegie-owned companies provided the iron ore and limestone, as well as even more coal for heating the furnaces. The mill was initially supplied with pig iron from Carnegie's nearby Lucy and Isabella furnaces, but a blast furnace added in 1880 made it possible to transform raw iron ore and coke into finished steel rails at one facility. By the end of the century, Carnegie Steel controlled the largest and richest deposits of coking coal and iron ore then known. Its Pittsburgh-area plants were the most modern in the world, with an annual output of 700,000 tons, more than that of Great Britain, and a profit in 1900 of $40 million.[29]

While wood retained its importance as a building material, the industrial achievements of the late nineteenth century were fueled by coal and, later, petroleum and natural gas. Mechanization, vertical integration, and consolidation of mining operations into larger and more heavily capitalized companies produced dramatic changes in the coalfields. This was true in both the anthracite-mining region of northeastern Pennsylvania and the bituminous coal areas of the state's west and south, where the arrival of the railroads provided access to remote areas of the Appalachian Mountains and drove demand. Coal operators, often subsidiaries or "captive mines" of steel or railroad corporations, built entirely new communities, known as "patch towns," to house workers and their families. The Leith Mine and Coke Works in Fayette County, for example, initially began operations in the 1880s to produce metallurgical coal for the Joliet Steel Company of Illinois. Frick bought the mine in 1889 and built the region's first steel tipple to hoist cars loaded with coal up the mine shaft and lower workers into the mine. Upon reaching the surface, workers loaded the coal into one of the "beehive" coking ovens that dotted the area to be slowly baked to remove impurities and increase carbon content before it was shipped to one of Carnegie's mills. By the start of the twentieth century, more than three hundred people worked in the mine and its adjacent coking facilities, producing more than 120,000 tons of coke annually.[30]

The development of the petroleum industry, too, created dramatic new working landscapes. The inventor and businessman Samuel Martin Kier established the nation's first refinery to produce illuminating oil from petroleum in Pittsburgh in 1853. On August 27, 1859, along Oil Creek in rural Venango County, north of the city, Edwin Drake, an agent for a group of Connecticut businessmen, oversaw drilling of the world's first underground petroleum well. The first shipment from Drake's well ignited an economic explosion that drew thousands of speculators to the Oil Region along the Allegheny River and its tributaries. The rule of capture, which determined that oil belonged to whomever brought it to the surface, caused the construction of hundreds of wells, often with little thought as to how to control the raw product once it began flowing. "Great difficulties arose from the want of barrels, which could not be made fast enough," one observer noted. "The owners of the wells tried to stop the flow of oil, but the wells would not cease to flow. 'Oil Creek' became literally what its name imported, for the oil was necessarily allowed to run to waste into the stream, the surface of which was covered with oil for miles."[31]

From pumping and transporting the crude to refining; storing and distributing petroleum products; and burning oil for light, heat, and propulsion to disposing of the waste products, every aspect of oil's life cycle created new working landscapes. Within the Oil Region, communities such as Pithole—which was laid out in May 1865, incorporated in December of that year with approximately twenty thousand residents, and had collapsed to fewer than three hundred residents by 1870—exemplified the fleeting nature of boom towns. By the late 1870s, John D. Rockefeller's Standard Oil Company had captured 90 percent of the nation's oil-refining capacity, much of which he located in Cleveland rather than Pittsburgh due to the former's location along multiple interstate railroad lines. The development of iron pipelines allowed Philadelphia, too, to become a major center of the oil industry, with its refining capacity growing from just over two thousand barrels a day in 1873 to more than twenty thousand by 1888 and nearly fifty thousand by 1897. Even as the state's heyday as the world's leading oil producer passed, the Atlantic Refining Company's colossal facility along the Schuylkill River was processing nearly 50 percent of the world's illuminating fuel by 1891 and 35 percent of all U.S. petroleum exports.[32]

———

Scholars often refer to regions where environmental quality is disregarded to provide cheap and abundant resources for distant areas as "sacrifice zones." This definition certainly applied to large swaths of Pennsylvania, where the working landscapes of oil, coal, and timber production resulted in clear-cut mountainsides, smoke-filled skies, and polluted waterways. The material gains of the industrial revolution were substantial, but it is important to keep in mind that, in the coal patches, lumber camps, and mill towns, the exploitation of the natural world went together with the abuse of human workers who often toiled long hours for low pay in miserable conditions. A series of environmental catastrophes and violent labor confrontations in the late nineteenth century drew attention to these problems as new social movements emerged to attempt to address them.[33]

3

CONSERVATION IN
THE KEYSTONE STATE

N EARLY 1886, motivated by the public lectures of Dr. Joseph Rothrock, a botanist and physician at the University of Pennsylvania, Maria Coxe and Mary Lundy convened a group of fellow elite Philadelphia women to discuss forest destruction. Lundy, the wife of a prominent Episcopalian minister with whom she vacationed regularly in New York State's Adirondack Mountains, later wrote in the group's magazine, *Forest Leaves*, that they were "impelled by the increasing destruction of the noble forests of Pennsylvania, to some concerted action in the way of forest preservation and the replanting of waste lands." After a few sessions at the Coxe home, they called a public meeting for May 26 at the Hall of the Historical Society of Pennsylvania, where Rothrock; Bernard Fernow, chief of the Forestry Division of the U.S. Bureau of Agriculture; and other experts addressed the crowd. By the end of the gathering, the group had agreed to form an organization that in June was officially named the Pennsylvania Forestry Association (PFA). The conservation era in Pennsylvania had officially begun.[1]

Accelerated exploitation of natural and human resources produced not only enormous wealth for a few but also social and environmental problems that threatened the cultural and material foundation of the commonwealth and nation. In response, a new generation of civic and political leaders, many of whom had roots in the Mid-Atlantic, mobilized to protect natural resources and sites of aesthetic beauty and historical significance. The most recognized of these conservationists, Gifford Pinchot, became the first chief of the U.S. Forest Service under Theodore Roosevelt and later created the model for what would become the Civilian Conservation Corps (CCC) while serving his second term as governor of Pennsylvania. In addition to the development of new state agencies and regulations designed to protect woods, waters, and wildlife, local communities mobilized to clean up working landscapes that had become inhospitable and even hazardous to human and nonhuman life.

City Beautiful

Industrialization and rapid population growth in Pennsylvania's cities, towns, and suburbs reshaped the natural world. Disease outbreaks and declining environmental quality prompted calls for new water and sewer infrastructure, the removal of farm animals from city streets, and the creation of recreational parks. Municipal reformers often included explicitly environmental elements in their agenda, such as Philadelphia's Fairmount Park Art Association, founded in 1872. Indeed, Harrisburg's J. Horace McFarland, who went on to lead the American Civic Association, wrote to his friend and fellow conservationist Mira Lloyd Dock in 1900, "I shall mildly point the finger of scorn at the potato parings on the river bank, the dump heap at the cemetery entrance, and a few other spots most apparent every day all about." As cities became increasingly engineered landscapes, environmental rehabilitation dovetailed with calls for cultural preservation, especially sites deemed to be of special importance to national identity, such as Valley Forge, which was established as Pennsylvania's first state park in 1893. By the early twentieth century, various reform groups interested in improving the urban landscape had coalesced loosely under the banner of "City Beautiful"—a movement with transatlantic roots that sought to achieve moral and civic virtue through environmental improvement.[2]

While each had their own individual characteristics, late nineteenth-century Pennsylvania communities followed the same basic pattern. The original urban core along a river or stream served as the commercial hub, surrounded by older neighborhoods that might have once been fashionable but had seen their populations move to new, more distant residential areas. In the place of middle- and upper-class residents, migrants from rural farms, Black people suffering from discrimination in employment and housing, and new immigrants from eastern and southern Europe filled the shabby tenements within walking distance of factories, where they scraped together a living. The relative lack of natural barriers to expansion enabled Philadelphia to spread easily to the north, south, and west, for example, especially following the construction of four new bridges across the Schuylkill River. The development of the streetcar and then the electric trolley in the 1890s allowed residents of even relatively modest means to live farther from their workplaces. Finally, the advent of structural steel, safety elevators, electric lighting, and other new technologies marked the rise of the skyscraper as downtown real estate prices pushed commercial buildings higher. In 1894, the addition of its famous statue of William Penn made Philadelphia's City Hall the tallest building in the world; by 1900, fifteen- to twenty-story buildings were increasingly common elements of the city's skyline.[3]

Urban politics were largely controlled by political machines (mostly Republican) in which elected leaders traded jobs and other favors for votes in working-class wards while they skimmed profits from water, sewer, and other infrastructure projects in neighborhoods that could pay for them. The Pittsburgh public works director Edward Bigelow, who never escaped the taint of association with a political machine controlled by his cousin Christopher Magee, wrote in 1890 that the "old wards of our city are very rapidly being turned into manufacturing sites and thereby forcing the residents thereof to locate in the East End in outer wards. Having once established their homes there, they very naturally and very properly ask [for] such streets and sewer improvements as well as water supplied as will make their lives accessible and healthful." Between 1888 and 1899, the city laid 190 miles of new sewers, graded ninety-four miles of city streets, and repaired twenty-two miles of streets with asphalt and fifty-five miles with block stone, most cut from the Ligonier quarries of Magee's business partner William Flinn.[4]

Basing calculations on lining their own pockets and controlling votes rather than improving environmental services and health outcomes for residents, machine politicians and their allies targeted water and sewer lines to favored neighborhoods, delayed constructing additional reservoirs, rejected water filtration proposals, and ignored deteriorating water quality. In 1903, the journalist Lincoln Steffens called Philadelphia "corrupt and contented," with the machine's kickbacks and crooked real estate deals connected intimately to the city's physical environment and health of residents. In Harrisburg, McFarland decried the indifference of a machine-led City Council as he emphasized the danger of drinking unfiltered water "after it had received the sewage of twenty-four (upriver) cities and towns" and called the resulting deaths from typhoid fever "municipal murder." Crowded immigrant neighborhoods increasingly suffered from a lack of open space for children to play. Upon a visit to a Philadelphia tenement district during the 1918 influenza epidemic, one observer noted the "unspeakably filthy conditions" where tenants were "obliged to live in surroundings which a farmer would not tolerate for one moment in his cow stable."[5]

The urban environmental reform program that came to be known as City Beautiful emerged out of a broader critique of industrial society by "Progressives," a political and social movement that generally embraced industrialization and capitalism but advocated for government involvement in ensuring a more equitable distribution of the benefits. Support for an expansion of public services and environmental regulation had slowly built, but during the 1890s new civic organizations advocated for a host of policy interventions, including expanded public education; improved housing and working conditions; and effective sewer, water, street, and other urban infrastructure. Parks, playgrounds, street cleaning, and tree planting efforts were connected to the belief that a wholesome physical environment enabled a moral citizenry and community success. Women were key actors as they mobilized social norms that associated femininity with domestic duties. Dock, for example, gave numerous speeches encouraging participation in the public parks movement as a means of providing "physical rest and moral uplifting" and likened urban environmental cleanup to "better housekeeping out of doors."[6]

A lecture by Dock at the Board of Trade in December 1900 titled "The City Beautiful" resulted in outrage at the reluctance of Harrisburg city officials to hike taxes for civic improvements and prompted reformers to develop their own proposals. The New York City sanitation expert James Fuertes advised building a low dam on the Susquehanna and deepening Paxton Creek for flood control, as well as installing a filtration system, expanding sewers, and building a reservoir. Warren H. Manning, a protégé of Frederick Law Olmsted, recommended enlarging Reservoir Park and transforming the Susquehanna Riverfront and several islands into parkland. Manning also endorsed "a great country park" at Wetzel's Swamp "framed in with wooded bluffs on the one side, and a line of fine old willows along the [Main Line] canal on the other."[7]

Civic reformers in smaller communities, too, embraced the Progressive spirit, working to reshape the urban landscape into a more wholesome form. In June 1898, Gertrude Bosler Biddle, a close friend of Dock's, gathered thirty-two women to form the Carlisle Civic Club, whose "first point of attack was the dirty streets." Biddle bemoaned that "broad thoroughfares and the open squares that William Penn had bestowed upon our forefathers gave evidence of much civic carelessness." Club women enlisted newspapers, secured anti-littering ordinances, installed trash cans, and hired a street sweeper, "with the result that, after five years of persistent agonizing, our streets are—improved." In addition to a host of activities, which included encouraging "love of flowers . . . shade and fruit trees" provided free or at low cost to schoolchildren, the club was working by 1903 to transform a "large plot of ground, well located, with handsome trees" into a public park.[8]

Progressive ideology emphasized volunteerism, but substantial improvements required public investment that could come only through municipal bonds. However, control of city halls required coalition building across class and ethnic lines to marshal votes and overcome powerful and entrenched political machines. This was no easy task. In Philadelphia, City Beautiful advocates were largely high-minded Republican elites, who "spoke mostly with one another and made little attempt to reach out to immigrants and workers." As a result, their only major electoral victory came in 1911 when a factional dispute within the machine allowed Rudolph Blankenberg to narrowly capture the Mayor's Office. The Blankenberg administration undertook overdue and necessary improvements, including eliminating street-level railroad crossings, starting construction on the Frankford Elevated and North Broad Street subway lines, and erecting new piers, but the mayor's political naivety and unwillingness to embrace patronage meant the machine's return to power in 1915.[9]

In Harrisburg, too, City Beautiful advocates faced an entrenched political machine with little incentive to challenge the status quo. In 1901, supporters of the "Harrisburg Plan" succeeded in getting a $1 million bond issue on the ballot and convinced the local businessman Vance McCormick to run against a machine candidate who refused to endorse environmental improvement. Launching what McFarland termed "a comprehensive and somewhat sensational campaign of education," supporters published newspaper articles; delivered tracts to every home; and gave talks to every club, group, and church that they could. Civic Club women visited schools with "a simple and admirable gospel of improvement" so children would encourage their fathers to support the bond and reform candidates. Finally, they emblazoned a trolley car with the message: "Vote for Pure Water, Better Sewers, playgrounds for children. DON'T GIVE OUR TOWN A BLACK EYE." Their work paid off, with the bond issue passing by a wide margin and reform candidates winning the offices of mayor, treasurer, and comptroller.[10]

By October 1905, Harrisburg residents were drinking filtered water years before Pittsburgh (1907) and Philadelphia (1911) fully implemented their own systems, while the new Susquehanna River low dam and sewer interceptor alleviated the raw sewage flowing into adjacent waterways. Flush with success, McFarland and Dock promoted the "Harrisburg Plan" throughout the state and nation, including in the "Beautiful America" column McFarland wrote for the *Ladies' Home Journal*. In 1902 he was elected president of the American Park and Outdoor Art Association and, following its 1904 merger with a similar organization, served as president of the new American Civic Association for twenty years. Dock worked especially through the Pennsylvania Federation of Women and the General Federation of Women's Clubs. These clubs existed in every region of the state and, as in Carlisle, often emphasized environmental improvement through street cleaning; garbage disposal; park construction; and tree, shrub, and flower planting. Indeed, McFarland noted that there was "no definitely successful civic betterment movement" that "was not actively promoted by the women of the community."[11]

Thousands of residents, from Philadelphia and Pittsburgh to smaller cities such as Harrisburg and Wilkes-Barre and modest boroughs such as Carlisle and West Chester, worked to alleviate the social and environmental strains of industrial society, but they faced a daunting task. Infrastructure improvements required maintaining the cross-class coalitions necessary to win majorities in municipal elections over many years. Further, many projects necessitated difficult-to-obtain changes to state laws and were frequently expensive, with resulting arguments over funding. Despite the completion of a water filtration plant in Pittsburgh in 1907, for example, landlords often refused to connect poor tenants to water lines, sewers, or electricity. Similarly, in 1913 state legislators finally outlawed some of the egregious practices found in mostly immigrant urban slums, but Philadelphia's City Council, beholden to real estate interests, refused to fund housing inspectors. Finally, in Harrisburg, as other communities, the benefits of City Beautiful often accrued along racial and class lines. Installing roads, water systems, parks, and the new Capitol complex required McFarland and other advocates to make compromises that, among others, resulted in destruction of the city's Old Eighth Ward (Figure 3.1) and dislocation of its disproportionately poor, immigrant, and Black residents. In 1911, one senator declared the Capitol's beauty "marred by the frightful setting in which the gem is placed. It is like a diamond set in lead." A decade later, the neighborhood's last property had been razed as construction commenced on Capitol Park.[12]

Figure 3.1 Old Eighth Ward, Harrisburg, looking northwest toward the State Capitol building, ca. 1907. (Courtesy: Pennsylvania State Archives, J. Horace McFarland Papers, MG-85.)

Conserving Forests and Waters

Even as the negative consequences of industrial society prompted urban reform, many Progressives turned their attention to the environmental problems of rural America. Women played pivotal roles in both contexts. Members elected Rothrock president of the PFA, and its founding officers were all men, for example, but much of the organization's energy and success in protecting forests, cleaning up polluted streams, and enforcing new game laws came from dense networks of female civic reformers. Dock, a university-trained botanist known for popular talks on wildflowers before she came to national attention as a civic reformer, had been Rothrock's friend since the 1870s and knew Coxe and Lundy from the State Federation of Pennsylvania Women. Dock quickly joined the PFA, and her Board of Trade lecture that helped launch Harrisburg's City Beautiful campaign came after she returned from a highly publicized trip to Europe, during which she studied under Sir Dietrich Brandis, the German forester who also mentored Pinchot. In 1901, Governor William A. Stone appointed Dock to the Forest Commission; she was the first woman to hold any statewide office in Pennsylvania and the world's first female forest commissioner.[13]

Successive waves of lumbering had swept across Pennsylvania's forests, so by 1895, out of a land base of 44,817 square miles, at least 4,716 square miles had become "wholly waste or worse" (Figure 3.2). Four thousand more square miles of farmland had been abandoned, partially due to soil infertility from deforestation and flooding. Dry brush from clear-cutting fueled enormous wildfires, and the resulting erosion threatened supplies of clean drinking water. Cultural attitudes and public policies encouraged these problems, as many local governments taxed developed properties at lower rates than undeveloped land. Colonial-era laws placed blame for damage caused by livestock on owners of unfenced property, with the result that enormous amounts of wood were still used for fence posts and railings. Finally, new transportation technologies that could ship products cheaply over long distances created competition that made farming marginal land in many parts of the state no longer profitable, pushing families off the land and to industrial cities.[14]

One strand of Progressive thinking about the broad consequences of industrial lumbering led to development of professional forestry to conserve resources for future generations. The widespread dissemination of George Perkins Marsh's *Man and Nature* (1864) linked deforestation to soil erosion and floods. In 1875, a small group of horticulturists and European-trained foresters created the American Forestry Association (AFA) to promote forest

Figure 3.2 W. T. Clarke, "Ready for Another Load. Hammersley Region, Northwestern Clinton Co., PA." (Courtesy: Pennsylvania State Archives, Clarke images, #3931, RG-6.)

conservation, and the U.S. Department of Agriculture hired its first special forestry agent. The AFA organized the first American Forestry Conference in Cincinnati in 1882, the same year that New York businessmen began lobbying to conserve Adirondack Mountain forests to protect the Hudson and Mohawk river headwaters, which fed the Erie Canal and thus served the economic interests of downstream cities. In 1885, New York's legislature created the nation's first State Forest Preserves in the Adirondack and Catskill mountains, a move later enshrined in the state's constitution.[15] This conservationist ethic made a significant impression on many middle- and upper-class Pennsylvanians, especially Pinchot and others who had strong economic and cultural ties to New York. While Pinchot's ancestral home was in Milford, Gifford's father, James, made his fortune as an interior design merchant in New York City and married the daughter of one of its wealthiest real estate developers. Gifford himself grew up shuttling among various family residences and spent portions of his summers in the Adirondacks, including one excursion in 1879 to Upper Ausable Pond, where he discovered a "new and lasting conception of the wilderness." When he returned from studying forestry in Europe in 1891, Pinchot accepted a position at Cornelius Vanderbilt's Biltmore Estate in North Carolina, where he sought to introduce scientific management practices and established what is considered the nation's first informal school of practical forestry. Pinchot later summed up his conservationist outlook as providing "the greatest good to the greatest number for the longest run," a philosophy that came to define the utilitarian approach to natural resource management.[16]

New York State's 1894 constitution declared that "the forest preserve as now fixed by law, shall be forever kept as wild forest lands. They shall not be leased, sold or exchanged, or be taken by any corporation, public or private, nor shall the timber thereon be sold, removed or destroyed." This preservationist language suggests a second strand of Progressive thought—an emerging spiritual ethos of wilderness as God's creation that existed in tandem with the more practical, resource-oriented ethic. This changing view of a benign and nurturing "nature" that needed protection from human excess was inspired, in part, by landscape painters such as Thomas Cole, who trained and exhibited at the Pennsylvania Academy of the Fine Arts in Philadelphia before moving to New York City. Cole and his contemporaries launched what became known as the Hudson River School, which focused on romantic depictions of pastoral scenes situated in obvious contrast to the dynamism of industrial cities. "They were lessons," in the words of the historian David Stradling, "on how to view nature, how to frame a picturesque vista, [and] how to appreciate the power of God by contemplating wild landscapes."[17]

Mary Lundy's husband, the Reverend John Patterson Lundy, was a prominent abolitionist and writer who emphasized this notion of bodily and spiritual regeneration through nature. Following a "breakdown in his health," he spent the winter of 1877–1878 in the Adirondacks, an experience he detailed in *The Saranac Exiles* (1880). Writing from the shores of Tupper Lake, Reverend Lundy explained that "here the church doors are always open; the grand cathedral aisles are full of light and beauty so soft and entrancing as to fill the soul with child-like delight, leading up as they do along the mighty columns of evergreen life to the vast blue apse of heaven." While receiving less attention than Pinchot, Rothrock, or even Dock, the Lundys were steadfast supporters of Pennsylvania's conservation movement. Mary served as the PFA's corresponding secretary for decades and coordinated with the statewide network of women's and civic clubs. For his part, John served as the organization's president from January 1891 until his death in December 1892 at sixty-nine. Trees "are meant for the double purpose of soul and body," he declared to the annual meeting, "that is for the instruction and discipline as well as for utility."[18]

While there were some precursors, such as William Penn's famous exhortation to "leave one acre of trees for every five acres cleared," the era of forest conservation in Pennsylvania really dates only to the 1880s. Indeed, the first state agency to develop out of the concern over industrial development focused not on forests, but on fish. Shad were first of the migratory species to appear in rivers each spring and one of the most important food sources for Native Americans and European colonists. Dam construction blocked shad from accessing more than 80 percent of their natural spawning grounds, while pollution and overfishing by commercial harvesters meant that in 1872 fisheries on the Delaware River above Milford yielded only a single fish. Alarmed by the depletion of shad in the Susquehanna and Delaware rivers, and of trout in mountain lakes and streams, the Pennsylvania legislature appointed James Worrell its first state fish commissioner in 1866. Worrell's recommendations quickly became laws requiring fishways and sluices on the state's major riverways and restricting the use of fish baskets, weirs, and other traps. In 1873, the legislature established a board of three fish commissioners to plan the systematic restoration of shad on the state's rivers.[19]

Concern over fish populations dovetailed with increasing worries about the quality of drinking water. In the late 1860s, the Pennsylvania legislature passed a series of laws that established the Fairmount Park Commission and enlarged the area under its control to ensure "an open public space and park, for the health and enjoyment of the citizens, and the preservation of the purity of the water supply to the City of Philadelphia." The commission acquired nearly three thousand acres along a thirteen-mile corridor of Wissahickon Creek and the Schuylkill River, creating the country's largest urban park. However, Philadelphia did not have the economic power of New York City, and no single waterway connected the major cities of Pennsylvania in the way that the Erie Canal linked New York State. The political consensus necessary to set aside vast swaths of rural land primarily to serve the interests of city residents as was done in the Adirondacks never emerged in the commonwealth. As a result, despite the protection of thousands of acres in Fairmount Park, John Lundy described the waters of the Schuylkill in 1880 as "disgusting, having a bilge-water odor."[20]

Increasing alarm over the inability to protect Philadelphia's drinking water and the growing interest in the role of scientific forestry among the city's civic elite thus provides important context for the creation and subsequent success of the PFA. Following its founding in 1886, the organization grew quickly and gained influence on both the state and national level. Within a year, the group had grown to 450 members at a time when the American Forestry Congress had only 139 and raised funds to send Rothrock on a statewide tour that brought scenes of forest destruction to urban residents. Finally, in 1893 the notoriously parsimonious state legislature authorized a study to explore a forestry commission, with Rothrock appointed as its head. Shortly after the report was delivered, the General Assembly created a Department of Agriculture and included in it a commissioner of forestry, as well as funding for a system of forest reserves. That same year, the state took control of Valley Forge, creating Pennsylvania's first state park.[21]

From 1898 to 1910, the state acquired 924,798 acres, almost half of the total acreage in the current state forest system. The creation of state forests highlighted the need for trained staff, but even by 1903 the Society of American Foresters had only fifteen member foresters. Following her appointment to the Forestry Commission in 1901, Dock dedicated herself to researching and then lobbying for the establishment of a forestry school. In 1903, Rothrock and Dock succeeded in convincing the legislature to establish the Pennsylvania State Forest Academy at Mont Alto in what would become the Michaux State Forest. The school opened its doors in July 1903 with full tuition and room and board covered and the state forester George Wirt serving as director. Ralph Brock, who was among the first Black people to study botany at the University of Pennsylvania, enrolled in the academy's first class with Rothrock's encouragement.[22]

Implementing conservation laws required balancing government authority with the desires of residents to continue customary practices, including hunting. Wildlife protection followed a similar trajectory to that of fishing, with county-level limits on harvesting birds and game animals beginning in the 1830s and state legislation emerging in the 1860s and 1870s. Finally, in 1895 the legislature established the Pennsylvania Game Commission (PGC) to enforce game laws and hired the first game protectors two years later. However, disciplining a population long used to hunting and fishing for food, as well as sport, was not easy. In 1904, for example, "Big Joe" Berrier, a muscular, six-foot-tall warden from Harrisburg described as being as "strong as two or three ordinary men," attempted to make five arrests in Luzerne County "a week or so prior to the opening of the game season." According to Joseph Kalfbus, the PGC's first executive secretary, "in four he met with armed resistance, and was compelled to use extreme force in making three of the arrests, knocking two of the men down, and shooting the hat off the head of a third." In 1921, William E. Shoemaker, who had earlier worked for the PGC, was shot attempting to apprehend two men spearfishing at night without a license in Bradford County. Shoemaker was the state's first fish warden to be killed in the line of duty.[23]

Class and ethnic identities shaped the rights of individuals to access natural resources on public lands. In 1902, the PGC established a restricted nonresident hunting license to "discourage hunting by people who weren't

Pennsylvanians"; in practice, this mostly meant recent immigrants from eastern and southern Europe. "From the time spring opens and our migratory birds begin to return, until that time comes again, they are at it, with guns, and traps, and snares, and every conceivable method, whereby living creatures can be killed or captured," Kalfbus complained, condemning immigrants hunting for sustenance using many of the same practices as earlier settlers. "Hardly a week passes without an assault of some kind on our officers, from these people," he reported. "More than one-half of all complaints that come to us of violations of the game laws, implicate in some way people of this class." Finally, in 1909 the legislature made it illegal for "unnaturalized, foreign-born residents" of Pennsylvania to own or possess shotguns or handguns. Notices were printed and circulated throughout the state in English, Slavic, and Italian advising immigrants of the new law, which was upheld in federal court in 1914 and not repealed until 1967.[24]

State forests, too, became battlegrounds for control of traditional uses of rural working landscapes. In an 1896 report, for example, Rothrock found the third most common reason for forest fires in Pennsylvania was "to clear away underbrush and so to encourage large berry crops in years immediately ensuing." This deliberate use of fire to support berry harvests, which echoed earlier Native American methods, apparently continued as a popular local practice until at least the 1920s, despite fines and suppression efforts by fire wardens. In 1901, the first ranger was appointed to police forest reserves in Pike County, and Commissioner George H. Wirt described a trip that year: "We knew that wood was being stolen from these lands, particularly barrel hoops, railroad ties and things of that kind—small stuff that could be easily handled. . . . Dr. Rothrock gave me the job to see if I could get the fellows who were stealing the timber." Further, commissioners at first informally allowed property owners near forest reservations free grazing rights for their cattle, but this privilege was persistently abused, in the view of state officials, by overgrazing. Finally, in 1906 the commission added "Rule 17," requiring permission to use public forests for agriculture and placing grazing lands under state control.[25]

Setting aside forest reserves and training foresters coincided with a broader movement in Pennsylvania society focused on environmental beautification, especially through tree and flower planting. John Bartram and his contemporaries had inspired a long history of aesthetic gardening in Pennsylvania, with the nation's first horticultural society established in Philadelphia in 1829. Horticulture proved particularly popular among women, who drew on European traditions of gendered responsibility for family gardens. In 1911, Jane Bowne Haines established the Pennsylvania School of Horticulture for Women, among the first of its kind, in Ambler, just north of Philadelphia. "Our vision," she declared, "was of a place where earnest-minded women could live and dream, where they should not be expected to do household work but should give their whole time to learning under competent teachers to become competent workers."[26]

Progressive women such as Haines, Dock, and Biddle parlayed the social acceptability of gardening into a central role as urban landscapers through the City Beautiful movement. The state's first systematic tree plantings, begun in 1899 and consisting of one thousand Carolina poplar, failed due to poor soils, competition from other trees, and repeated fires at their test plot in Pike County. At the urging of Dock, the forestry commission then set up a nursery at Mont Alto under Brock's direction, where the first successful plantings happened in 1902; by 1909, 5.8 million tree seedlings were growing in state nurseries. At the same time, a series of public laws authorized shade tree commissions throughout the state and provided tax rebates for landowners who protected trees planted along roadsides with fences. Municipalities were permitted to pass ordinances to protect trees, and the cities of Pittsburgh, York, and Wilkes-Barre formed commissions, as did eleven smaller communities. By 1923, 34.9 million trees had been planted on state and private lands.[27]

While Progressivism as a national political movement waned during the 1920s, Pennsylvania continued expanding the state's role in conserving fish, wildlife, water, and forests. In 1923, during Pinchot's first term as governor, the legislature consolidated the Department of Forestry, the Water Supply Commission, and the Bureau of Topographic and Geologic Survey into a new Department of Forests and Waters, with a broad mission of protecting and conserving natural resources. That same year, the federal government created the Allegheny National Forest on more than 500,000 square acres around the upper reaches of the Allegheny River. Almost immediately the Automobile Club of Philadelphia touted this cut-over wilderness of northwestern Pennsylvania as "a marvelous national park within easy reach of Pennsylvania motorists."[28]

Despite these efforts to conserve and restore Pennsylvania's forests, trees continued to be clear-cut; wildfires still raged; and working landscapes faced new threats from invasive species. The most notorious of these, the chestnut blight, virtually eliminated mature chestnut trees in less than a generation from forests that they previously dominated. The demands of World War I also caused an upsurge in industrial production, mining, and lumbering. During the 1920s, industrial pollution worsened, devastating floods continued, and the threat of waterborne disease endured. Further, environmental amenities remained unevenly distributed, with poor people, new immigrants, and people of color often confined to the dirtiest, most dangerous jobs and unhealthiest, most polluted neighborhoods. Indeed, even Brock faced enormous prejudice, according to one of his classmates, "for none of the boys could quite content himself being ordered around by a darky, regardless of his ability." Brock left his position at the Forest Academy in 1911 and never worked as a state forester again. Instead, he eventually moved to New York City and served as a landscape gardener at the new Radio City complex and for several high-profile (and segregated) developments, including the Paul Laurence Dunbar Apartments and the Harlem River Houses, the first public housing complex built with federal funds.[29]

A New Deal for Nature

On June 5, 1933, a convoy of military trucks stopped at a clearing along a nondescript forest road in Rothrock State Forest near the ridge of Tussey Mountain in Centre County. A group of sleep-deprived young Black men, mostly from Philadelphia and nearby communities, stared at a pile of tents and other equipment. This marked the beginning of CCC Camp S-62. "To those of us who came up here last June into a mountain wilderness and endured the hardships of sleeping in floorless tents and bathing in a creek," Cheyney M. Thomas of Downingtown recalled, "well, it's somewhat of a soul-revisor to be able to see the results of eight months labor which finds our camp ninety-eight percent complete." The CCC, which remained segregated throughout its existence and prohibited women, represented the merger of conservation with economic relief that remade vast swaths of rural Pennsylvania as other New Deal programs transformed cities and towns. This new era of public spending on environmental infrastructure culminated with the opening in 1940 of the Pennsylvania Turnpike across the Appalachian Mountains, which served as the template for the Interstate Highway System and marked the automobile's ascendance.[30]

The crisis of the Great Depression began long before Wall Street's Black Friday crash in 1929. The number of Pennsylvania farms peaked in the twentieth century's first decade and began a sustained decline that did not slow until around 1970. The internal combustion engine allowed farmers to speed production and freed up millions of acres formerly needed for growing horse feed, but also required new spending on expensive equipment and fuel, not to mention increasing air pollution. Even as the average farm size increased from fewer than one hundred to more than 140 acres, more than nine million acres of agricultural land were taken out of production through reforestation or development. Farmers responded to high demand for foodstuffs during World War I through consolidation and mechanization, often funded by credit, only to suffer catastrophe and, frequently, foreclosure when the end of the war caused a collapse in food prices. As marginal land was abandoned, the state often stepped in at tax sales to add to forestry and game lands. Despite the temporary return of some unemployed urban workers to the countryside, by 1940 just 8 percent of Pennsylvania's population lived on farms.[31]

With unemployment surging, Pennsylvania voters turned again to Pinchot, whose now old-fashioned Progressive politics placed him closer to Democrats' New Deal vision of government expansion than Republican laissez-faire policies. In his second term as governor, Pinchot retained fiscal conservatism and teetotaling support for Prohibition, but also populist anger at what he described as "the most astounding concentration of wealth in the hands of a few men the world has ever known." Following the lead of his friend and political ally, New York Governor Franklin Roosevelt, Pinchot convinced the state legislature in November 1931 to appropriate $10 million for direct relief of unemployed residents. Also, like Roosevelt, who was elected president in November 1932, Pinchot used some of this limited state money for public works projects, including putting twenty-five thousand men to work building roads and 1,100 more cutting firewood for needy families.[32]

This modest intervention portended a change in federal and state spending on development projects, with major consequences for Pennsylvania's working landscapes. The existence of the Department of Forests and Waters along with the Allegheny National Forest meant that, when Pinchot's model for putting unemployed men to work on forestry projects was federalized through the CCC, Pennsylvania had both the need and the administrative framework to take immediate advantage. On April 3, 1933, before any specific plans had yet been established in Washington, DC, a crowd of two thousand young men converged on the employment bureau in downtown Philadelphia hoping to be selected for the program. The state's first CCC camp was operational by April 24 in the Allegheny National Forest, which made it second nationwide only to Camp Roosevelt in Virginia. "The first day was cold and rainy," recalled Henry Bier of Pittsburgh of the camp's founding. "Some of the guys had holes in their socks and some didn't have any socks and some had holes in their shoes." By July's end, there were eighty-nine CCC camps on state lands in Pennsylvania, including S-62, known as "Penn-Roosevelt" (Figure 3.3); seven in the Allegheny National Forest; and one at Gettysburg Military Park. Pennsylvania hosted ninety-seven CCC camps at its peak, by far the most of any eastern state and second only to California. All told, more than 194,000 men passed through the program

Figure 3.3 "CCC Camp Lined Up for Supper." Penn-Roosevelt CCC camp, May 25, 1933. (Courtesy: Pennsylvania State Archives, Emergency Conservation Work Photographs, RG-6.)

during its nine-year existence. "It was just wonderful," recalled Walter Traveny. "Kids who were in the streets had all they wanted to eat, all their clothes, and $30 a month."[33]

The primary purpose of the camps was conservation and historic preservation work, which also included road building to make remote sites accessible to the growing number of auto tourists. As S-62's William Bryant explained in the *Philadelphia Tribune*, "Young trees are being planted by a group of our boys who are becoming very specialized in this type of thing. Others are building roads over the mountains to facilitate the fighting of fire, and for general traffic through the forests." For Roosevelt and Pinchot, this work was necessary to repair damage inflicted on the forests by years of corporate greed and open them up to new types of commercial development. It was also intended to restore the mental and physical well-being of a generation of young men wracked by poverty and forced idleness. "Let's not forget those boys that swing axes all day—short, tall, skinny, fat, but all putting on muscles and growing into fine manhood," explained S-62's Cheyney Thomas. "One cannot appreciate the change that comes over boys in such a place." Indeed, for young men from Philadelphia, Pittsburgh, and other cities, this may have been their first time living away from an urban environment. Pinchot and allies in the forestry movement hoped they would leave the program supporting conservation policies. "The biggest thing was probably the learning that went on," recalled one supervisor during the fiftieth anniversary of the CCC's creation. "It built the foundation for a conservation ethic all through society that's still a factor today."[34]

By the program's end in 1942, Pennsylvania's CCC workers had strung 791 miles of telephone lines, planted more than sixty-one million trees, built or refurbished 3,386 miles of forest roads and 3,483 miles of foot and horse trails, and installed more than a hundred large dams. Much of this was undertaken in state parks that had begun being designated with Valley Forge in 1893 and Mont Alto, Promised Land, and Caledonia between 1902 and 1905. For decades, these sites were underfunded afterthoughts compared with state forests, but increasing automobile travel created demand for camping, picnic, and recreational facilities. Conservation and construction work of the CCC and other New Deal programs resulted in twenty-nine new state parks between 1930 and 1945 alone. "Huge logs are being laid [and] approximately 1000 truckloads of stone to fill the spaces between," the camp reporter noted of S-62 in 1935, along with "two large pavilions, several stone walks, camp stoves, a beautiful driveway around the Dam and numerous recreational items." Upon completion, he predicted, "'Penn-Roosevelt' will undoubtedly be the garden spot of this locality."[35]

Forest conservation was only part of massive federal expansion that had dramatic effects on working landscapes far from wooded backcountry. The CCC itself, for example, also undertook conservation of historic resources—most notably, at Gettysburg National Battlefield and Hopewell Furnace in Chester County, which in 1938 became one of the first National Historic Sites of the National Park Service (NPS). Like S-62, the segregated CCC camps under NPS supervision at Gettysburg were staffed by Black men under the supervision of White officers. In Philadelphia, other relief programs, such as the Works Progress Administration (WPA), reshaped an urban environment that was broadly seen as decaying. The city's Republican politicians initially refused to accept federal funding, viewing it as a challenge to the machine patronage system and even sending residents outside of the city for work relief programs. Soon, however, federal money for slum clearance, street repair, and public housing construction, sold largely as an opportunity for employment in building trades, began pouring in. The city's largest project connected the Ridge Avenue subway stop via high-speed electric rail across the Ben Franklin Bridge to Broadway Station in Camden, New Jersey. Along with smaller beautification and artistic projects, other New Deal programs included the construction of several schools, such as Central High; improvements to Fairmount Park and Independence Hall; and Philadelphia's first public housing project, the Carl Mackley Houses.[36]

New Deal public spending had a similarly profound effect on Pittsburgh's working landscape. Despite their conservatism, several key civic and business leaders embraced the opportunity to remake the urban environment, and a series of plans in the 1920s established a vision for clearing riverfronts and building highways. With the city's heavy industrial tax base shattered by the Depression, however, Pittsburgh officials had difficulty raising matching funds to take advantage of public works programs; in 1938, for example, the city barely scraped together $15,000 for a WPA tree-planting project. With its greater resources, Allegheny County sponsored the bulk of road and bridge programs, which literally paved the way for postwar suburban development. In 1939, business leaders invited the urban planner Robert Moses, primary architect of the New York State Parkway System, to design a system of roadways that relieved congestion downtown and connected the central business district to outlying areas. Soon the plan was set in motion to transform "The Point," the heavily developed area where the Allegheny and Monongahela joined to form the Ohio River, into a historical park from which a series of parkways would radiate to the east and west.[37]

From rural towns such as Greenville and Bellefonte to industrial satellites such as Turtle Creek, Sharpsburg, and Clairton and small cities such as Johnstown and Sharon, New Deal funding underwrote drainage culverts, hardened river embankments, and completed sanitary sewer systems. In Allentown, federal spending supported the construction of two giant reservoirs, which provided residents with "a plentiful supply of good water," as well as parks and riverfront parkways that continue to define the city's green spaces. "Probably it would have taken 50 years of slow progress to accomplish what has been done under WPA in two years," explained Robert J. Wheeler, secretary of the Allentown Planning Commission. On the other side of the spectrum, in tiny Shoemakersville, Berks County, population 937, "water and sanitary sewer lines were installed . . . for the first time," also thanks to the WPA.[38]

The highest-profile and most celebrated statewide building project of the New Deal era was the "superhighway" across the Appalachian Mountains that established a model for postwar interstate highways. Pinchot campaigned for his second run as governor in 1931 on a platform that promised to "get the farmer out of the mud." At the time, nearly three-quarters of the state's 100,000 miles of roads were the responsibility of small townships that largely lacked resources to improve highways for automobile use. Once elected, Pinchot asked the legislature to take over some twenty thousand of these rural roads, which was done without a dissenting vote. The state quickly put unemployed men to work building a network of improved "Pinchot Roads" that proved a boon to farmers, as well as to myriad small villages and towns. Along with paving, roadways saw their width and ability to sustain heavy use increased, setting the stage for cars to replace walking and horsepower for individual transportation and trucks to replace trains for hauling goods. Between 1935 and 1961, the total number of registered vehicles in the state more than doubled, from 1,852,249 to 4,370,084 autos, trucks, and buses.[39]

Expanding on these local improvements, the WPA appropriated $35,000 in 1935 to survey the possibility of building a limited access highway across the state along the abandoned South Penn Railroad corridor. State officials received $26 million from the federal Public Works Administration and then a loan from the Reconstruction Finance Corporation in 1938. In about two years, crews built 160 miles over the mountains between Carlisle and Irwin at less than 3 percent grade, including almost three hundred bridges and seven tunnels. The Pennsylvania Turnpike opened at midnight on October 1, 1940, with motorists already queued at either end; during its first fifteen days of operation, "America's First Superhighway," as boosters branded it, saw more than 150,000 vehicles. The new road cut travel time between Pittsburgh and Harrisburg from nearly six hours to just two and a half, providing a direct link between the Mid-Atlantic and Midwest. More than 2.4 million vehicles would soon travel the "Granddaddy of the Pikes" each year, presaging a massive reorganization of the state's working landscapes around the automobile.[40]

––––––––

By the time Pennsylvanians began mobilizing for World War II, the Progressive conservation movement had made significant strides in easing some of the strains caused by industrialization. Working landscapes in cities, towns, and rural areas benefited from new laws and, perhaps, an emerging appreciation of the fragility of the ecosystems on which human society depended. Nevertheless, the reindustrialization of the 1940s underscored continuing problems of air and water pollution, while the increased government support for highways such as the Pennsylvania Turnpike heralded a new era of postwar suburbanization that would soon place enormous pressures on the state's environment.

4

ENVIRONMENTAL MOVEMENTS

ER FRIEND CALLED IT THE "POISON BOOK" due to a tone and subject matter that departed radically from her previous award-winning nature writing, but the publication of Rachel Carson's *Silent Spring* in September 1962 heralded the birth of the environmental protection movement. It opened with a depiction of the changing seasons of a community "in the midst of a checkerboard of prosperous farms, with fields of grain and hillsides of orchards" that resembled her hometown of Springdale, northeast of Pittsburgh along the Allegheny River. After years of living in harmony with the natural world, she wrote, "a strange blight crept over the area and everything began to change." Birds and bees died; children suffered from a mysterious illness; and vegetation grew brown and withered "as though swept by fire." The culprit was not witchcraft or enemy action, Carson concluded; the "people had done it themselves" (Figure 4.1).[1]

Pennsylvania's environment faced both new and ongoing threats in the decades following World War II. In addition to pesticides and other chemicals that Carson described as saturating the natural world, rapid suburban development and intensifying industrialization fouled waterways with untreated sewage and skies with chimney smoke and automobile exhaust. As farm fields and forests increasingly gave way to highways and housing developments, surface mining for coal scarred tens of thousands of acres and left some rural areas virtually uninhabitable. It also became clear that many historic urban neighborhoods were descending into economic obsolescence even as new immigrants and Black people sought better lives there. Environ-

Figure 4.1 Rachel Carson, official photograph, ca. 1943. (Courtesy: U.S. Fish and Wildlife Service.)

mental protection was thus part of several interconnected movements, spanning from wilderness conservation to civil rights and historic preservation, which sought to address the inequalities that manifested in the state's working landscapes.

These environmental movements emerged during a period of great material abundance in which consumption, especially of items related to home and family life, was seen as a patriotic duty. "Good citizenship and good consumerism were promoted as inseparable," the historian Lizabeth Cohen explained, "since economic recovery after a decade and a half of depression and war depended on a dynamic mass consumption economy." However, for many Pennsylvanians, economic growth that promised an ever increasing quality of life also came to threaten their health and well-being. Further, the Progressive-era assumption that the rest of the natural world should primarily serve human needs (even if conserved for future generations) proved increasingly inadequate. Instead, a new generation of scientists and activists embraced the concept of ecology, which placed humans within rather than above a complex and interconnected web of environmental relationships. "Man's attitude toward nature is today critically important simply because we have now acquired a fateful power to alter and destroy nature," Carson declared in 1963. "But man is a part of nature, and his war against nature is inevitably a war against himself." These tensions between consumption and conservation framed debates over how best to protect and use "the natural, scenic, historic, and esthetic values of the environment" for the remainder of the twentieth century and beyond.[2]

Bulldozers in City and Countryside

A visitor to southern Bucks County in 1955 would have encountered a radically different working landscape from that of just five years earlier. What had been a mostly rural community of truck farms was being rapidly replaced by a new suburban environment of single-family homes and roadways connecting them to Philadelphia. Between 1952 and 1958 the construction firm Levitt and Sons launched its second "Levittown" (the first was established on Long Island in 1947) and built 17,311 new homes at a maximum rate of one finished house every sixteen minutes (Figure 4.2). Of course, construction did not happen in an undisturbed wilderness; these had been agricultural working landscapes at least since the eighteenth century, but the intensity of new infrastructure increased impermeable surfaces of concrete and asphalt, buried streams, and concentrated human waste in unregulated septic tanks or community sewers emptying directly into waterways. New homeowners expecting to escape the city's dirt and grime had a rude awakening when their yards turned to rank, waste-filled marshes or runoff fouled local streams. For others, the loss of a nearby farm or woodlot to a new highway or housing subdivision undercut the bucolic ideal featured in the marketing that had drawn them to Levittown and other suburbs in the first place. This tension between consumers' expectations for natural amenities and the lived reality of unregulated development laid the foundation for the environmental movement.[3]

Pennsylvania cities that suburbanites left behind suffered their own environmental problems. Deforestation and intense development along rivers, for example, exacerbated unusual weather conditions in March 1936, resulting in the infamous St. Patrick's Day Flood that left 65 percent of Pittsburgh's central business district and one-third of the city of Johnstown under water. In the summer of 1946, Philadelphia officials dredged 500,000 tons of sludge from the silt-clogged Queen Lane and Roxborough reservoirs—neither had been cleaned since it opened in the 1890s—the first step in attempting to address the "chlorine cocktail" that resulted from trying to disinfect and mask the taste of one of the nation's dirtiest water supplies. Finally, in October 1948 an air inversion trapped emissions from U.S. Steel's Donora Zinc Works, the American Steel and Wire plant, and hundreds of other smaller

Figure 4.2 Aerial view of Levittown, 1952. (Courtesy: Temple University Libraries, Special Collections Research Center, McDowell *Evening Bulletin* Collection.)

sources close to the ground, killing twenty people, causing respiratory problems for thousands more, and resulting in one of the worst air pollution disasters in U.S. history.[4]

Even leaving aside extremes, day-to-day environmental problems increasingly called into question the viability of urban life, prompting political and industrial leaders to take radical steps to make their cities more attractive to investors and residents. Working-class residents and industrial elites alike were often ambivalent about the importance of controlling air pollution—smoke was often associated with prosperity in industrial society. Nevertheless, extreme pollution during World War II and the election of the Democrat David Lawrence as Pittsburgh's mayor paved the way for implementing a successful smoke control ordinance in 1946. The victory over smoke initiated a partnership between Lawrence and the business-backed Allegheny Conference on Community Development on a broader urban renewal effort, known as the Pittsburgh Renaissance, that sought to refashion the old industrial city for the automobile age. Over the next twenty years, officials cleared thousands of acres at the city's Point and along the three rivers to build a state park commemorating the city's origins, new office towers, and a series of highways to direct traffic to and from this new "Golden Triangle." Urban renewal beyond downtown also included the construction of new public housing and a civic arena.[5]

Inspired by Pittsburgh's public-private partnerships, business leaders in Philadelphia organized the Greater Philadelphia Movement in 1948 to address their city's problems. Over the next two decades, officials built new water and sewer plants; enhanced streets, bridges, and public transit lines; and modernized garbage collection. Three major projects in Center City, overseen by the influential urban planner Edmund Bacon, attracted the most attention and established the framework for the modern downtown. First, state and federal authorities demolished six square blocks around Independence Hall to create parking for tourists arriving by automobile. The Pennsylvania Railroad also razed its Broad Street Station and massive viaduct known as the "Chinese Wall," making way for an enormous mixed-use space called Penn Center. Finally, Bacon experimented with historic preservation as a development strategy by using eminent domain to transform an older area of commercial activity and deteriorating housing near the offices of Center City into "Society Hill," a gentrified neighborhood of mostly high-income, college-educated, White residents.[6]

It was not just Pennsylvania's largest cities that struggled to address erosion of commercial property values, or "blight" as it became commonly known. By 1960 a host of smaller communities had established comprehensive plans and planning commissions, created redevelopment authorities, and launched urban renewal programs of their own. The city of Lancaster was typical, with an aging housing stock that often lacked plumbing, heating, and utilities and "desperately needed modernization." However, as in Allentown, Reading, and other smaller cities, urban renewal in Lancaster could not achieve the level of political consensus and financial wherewithal that Philadelphia or Pittsburgh marshaled to demolish downtown areas and build infrastructure that could attract new service sector employers. Instead, civic elites largely targeted areas just outside of downtown, disproportionately demolishing areas with higher Black populations, often with little to show for it beyond vacant lots. Lancaster's principal commercial redevelopment project, which involved the demolition of most of the second block of North Queen Street, remained entirely vacant for a decade as officials struggled to attract a developer. The most conspicuous aspect of the effort, a retail and recreational project designed by the internationally famous architect Victor

Gruen known as Lancaster Square, was itself partly demolished only two years after its completion to make way for other new buildings.[7]

Urban renewal further concentrated poverty and distanced many residents, especially minorities, from parks and other natural amenities even as they were subjected to disproportionate levels of pollution from factories at which they were often not afforded equal employment. Fighting for what later became known as "environmental justice," civil rights advocates demanded the desegregation of community parks and fought to end racial discrimination that confined many Black residents to inadequate housing, unsafe working conditions, and unhealthy surroundings. Public swimming pools, for example, became flashpoints for both community activism and racialized violence. During the 1920s and 1930s, the primary focus of pools shifted from sanitation to recreation, and as large resort-style facilities were built in urban parks, men and women were increasingly able to use them together for the first time. As a result, long-standing racist concerns about socializing, especially among Black boys and White girls, prompted the segregation of these sites. In 1931, the opening of an enormous new outdoor swimming pool in Pittsburgh's Highland Park resulted in years of violence against Black swimmers repeatedly targeted by White mobs with the tacit support of police and local elected officials. Renewed attention to civil rights during and immediately after World War II culminated in a biracial effort to desegregate Pittsburgh's pools, resulting in a violent attack that required 160 police officers to quell. It was not until a lawsuit brought by activists in 1951 that city officials finally took steps necessary to desegregate the Highland Park pool. Meanwhile, throughout the city and state, other public pools remained closed to Black residents; as late as 1962, for example, a sign posted outside the West Penn Swimming Pool warned: "No dogs or [racial epithet] allowed."[8]

Rural areas throughout Pennsylvania experienced population loss, moribund employment opportunities, and erosion of environmental quality. Agriculture remained an important economic activity, though competition with western agribusiness made it increasingly difficult for small producers to remain self-sufficient. The farms that remained grew significantly in size and intensity of land use, with extensive use of nitrogen and phosphorus fertilizers that caused eutrophication and algal blooms in downstream bodies of water—most notably, the Chesapeake Bay and Lake Erie. In mining areas, the broader shift to fuel oil and other energy sources, along with advances in mechanization, dramatically reduced manpower needs and prompted a steady stream of migrants fleeing poverty and unemployment. The rapid increase of surface mining in many parts of the state left unproductive and unattractive land that affected both environmental quality and the social fabric of rural communities. Beneath it all, a poison legacy festered in hundreds of abandoned mines in the form of polluted water that affected an estimated three thousand miles of streams and continued to seep into waterways long after production ceased.[9]

Other rural areas closer to population centers, however, were being quickly transformed into suburbs. The rapid rate by which large swaths of so-called open space were developed for housing, industrial parks, airports, shopping centers, schools, and highways prompted a new generation of conservationists, many with ties to Pennsylvania, to advocate for setting aside natural areas and protecting scenic waterways. Howard Zahniser, the longtime executive of the Wilderness Society, for example, grew up along the banks of the Allegheny River near the Allegheny National Forest. In 1956, he authored the Wilderness Act, which was introduced in the House of Representatives by Republican Congressman John P. Saylor of Johnstown. A strong coal industry supporter as well as an avid fly fisherman, Saylor shepherded the Wilderness Act over the eight years it took to finally be signed into law by President Lyndon Johnson in 1964. Dubbed "St. John" by conservationists, Saylor also championed the Wild and Scenic Rivers Act for waterways that "possess outstandingly remarkable scenic, recreational, geologic, fish and wildlife, historic, cultural or other similar values" to "be preserved in free-flowing condition." In setting aside such areas, especially for recreation, Saylor and his contemporaries sought to better balance the demands of consumption and conservation.[10]

If Joseph Rothrock was the hero of Progressive-era conservation, Maurice Goddard carried this mantle from his appointment in 1955 as secretary of the Department of Forests and Waters through his retirement from state government in 1979. Wartime demand brought Pennsylvania's lumber industry back from a long decline that reached a nadir of only seventy-three million board feet in 1932—a more than 90 percent drop from its peak in 1899. The former director of the School of Forestry at Pennsylvania State University, Goddard understood the importance of sustainable timber production but increasingly emphasized recreation as motivation for additional land acquisition. Within months of confirmation, Goddard helped push through a law that assigned revenues from oil and gas leases on state lands for exclusive use in conservation, recreation, and flood control. With this additional funding in hand, he committed the department to "a state park within twenty-five miles of *every* resident of the Commonwealth," preferably with "a body of water" for swimming and boating. "Parks are for people," he declared. "Therefore, they should be located near where people live—near centers of great population concentration, but also near smaller communities."[11]

In 1955, Pennsylvania had approximately fifty state parks, including five historical parks, but many were carved from state forests and located in remote areas with few amenities. Goddard had thirteen new sites under development within two years, but annual park attendance tripled between 1955 and 1961 as the postwar boom provided additional leisure time and the ability to travel by car for millions of Americans, especially suburban White people. With demand for outdoor recreation outstripping supply, Goddard presented a plan for land acquisition and park development, especially in the forty-three counties where 90 percent of the state's people lived, to be funded through a $70 million bond issue. Sportsmen's groups, the travel industry, and civic clubs strongly backed the initiative, dubbed Project 70, which passed with overwhelming General Assembly support. However, the bond issue required a constitutional amendment and was opposed by many rural residents, presumably because they felt they had plenty of nearby land and saw no need to raise taxes to purchase more. Some industry groups feared that the expansion of state parks and focus on outdoor recreation might conflict with rural enterprises, especially farming and coal mining, and resented the potential use of eminent domain to acquire private property.[12]

Goddard crisscrossed the state with a "missionary approach" in 1963 to win the popular vote for Project 70 with a margin of only about 5 percent. Armed with this funding, the state added more than sixty thousand acres at seventeen new parks between 1964 and 1970. Nevertheless, visitation continued to soar, and it became clear that officials would need even more resources to ensure that parks were properly staffed and maintained, especially because Goddard and his fellow advocates insisted on free public access. Other types of working landscapes, too, had obvious needs too expensive to be handled at the local level, including drainage from abandoned coal mines and the expansion of municipal sewage treatment. In response the legislature passed, and voters affirmed by a two-to-one margin, a colossal $500 million bond issue creating the Land and Water Conservation and Reclamation Fund, signed by Republican Governor Raymond Shafer in January 1968. A new golden age for conservation had arrived, funded by the same economic growth that created new environmental challenges.[13]

An Environmental Revolution

Pennsylvania's worst mining disaster since World War II came not from fire but water and helped set the environmental movement's agenda. On January 22, 1959, Knox Coal Company workers breached the bottom of the Susquehanna River near Pittston, killing twelve men and causing underground flooding that spread from mine to mine throughout the Wyoming Valley. Ironically, the anthracite industry's collapse in the disaster's wake exacerbated pollution problems; as companies went bankrupt, pumps that prevented mine flooding shut down, allowing millions of gallons of acidified water to build up underground. In 1961, the Glen Alden Coal Company switched on three new deep-mine water pumps paid for by federal and state officials eager to restart the floundering industry. Within two days, the Susquehanna River from Wilkes-Barre to Sunbury was polluted with acidified water, killing an estimated 300,000 fish. "It was like tile on a floor, you couldn't walk near the river without stepping on dead fish," recalled Deborah Beck, whose father, Basse Beck, frequently drew attention to pollution in his newspaper column "Up and Down the River."[14]

If the publication of *Silent Spring* in 1962 helped an environmental movement to coalesce, it was because so many people like Basse Beck were already alarmed by these types of disasters.[15] Pennsylvania created its first Commissioner of Fisheries in 1866, and the 1905 Purity of Waters Act had been established "for the protection of the public health," but the focus was primarily on pollution abatement rather than prevention, and exemptions were always included for mining and other powerful industries. As a result, despite Fish Commission Secretary Albert Day's describing the event as "one of the more serious pollution problems we have ever faced" (it was the largest fish kill in the river's history), Glen Alden officials denied any wrongdoing and complained that the state Department of Health was harassing the company by insisting it treat mine water discharge. Ultimately, the company, the largest employer in Luzerne County with a payroll of $12 million, voluntarily "contributed" $45,000 to the Fish Commission to compensate for losses.[16]

The state already had a variety of conservation laws and a host of agencies, most established during the Progressive era, to oversee them. But these remained discrete areas of public policy, with no clear sense of an overarching "environment" that needed systematic protection, let alone an ecological ethic that provided legal protections beyond perceived human need. Anger over pollution problems, including a series of acidified water discharges of which the Glen Alden incident was only the largest, resulted in a remarkable period of legislative activity as the General Assembly passed tough new environmental laws related to surface and underground coal mining, air pollution, solid waste management, water pollution, scenic rivers, and environmental review in highway planning. In 1970 the state brought together many of its various agencies charged with environmental protection under a unified Department of Environmental Resources, and the following year voters overwhelmingly approved an amendment to the state constitution guaranteeing every Pennsylvanian a right to "clean air, pure water, and to the preservation of the natural, scenic, historic, and esthetic values of the environment."[17]

Two of the leaders of this "environmental revolution" in the General Assembly were Franklin Kury, who won election from Sunbury in 1966 with the slogan "Clean Politics, Clean Streams," and John Laudadio, a retired electrical engineer from Westmoreland County who was president of the Pennsylvania Federation of Sportsmen's Clubs. With broader public awareness of pollution problems and the power of coal interests on the wane, the Republican-dominated legislature had finally moved in 1965 to expand the state's Clean Streams law to include mine drainage. Indeed, Kury had used local anger over a vote against the law by his opponent, a long-serving Republican named Adam Bower, to win his seat. Besides passing modest bills that regulated coal refuse piles and open pit mining and joining the Susquehanna River Basin Compact with New York, Maryland, and the federal government, the most important environmental achievement of the 1967–1968 session was the creation of a Joint Legislative Air and Water Pollution Conservation Committee to track the performance of mine drainage remediation paid for by the new Land and Water Conservation and Reclamation Fund (also known as Project 500).[18]

While they remained in the political minority, Kury and Laudadio (both Democrats) used membership on the joint committee to plan an environmental agenda, particularly updating water pollution regulations. Fact-finding tours throughout the state's six major watersheds in late 1967 and 1968 exposed lawmakers, and those who followed the extensive newspaper coverage, to the problem's enormity, with expert testimony helping to establish a common framework for guiding discussions back in Harrisburg. As a result, when Laudadio was appointed chair of the Conservation Committee after Democrats took leadership of the House in 1969 (Kury was named committee secretary), they were ready to introduce a bill comprehensively rewriting the existing Clean Streams Law. Their efforts were joined by the joint committee's first director, Ralph Abele, a widely respected conservationist from Pittsburgh. Under Abele, the joint committee quickly acquired a broader sense of mission in providing direct assistance to the legislature in establishing a new environmental regulatory regime.[19]

Dealing with environmental pollution achieved a degree of bipartisan cooperation in the late 1960s on both the state and national level that has rarely been matched. Despite the far-reaching nature of the proposed new Clean Streams Law, which completely revised, rewrote, and expanded state control over water discharges two years before passage of the federal Clean Water Act, the House bill was introduced with sixty cosponsors and passed unanimously,

197–0. The Senate passed a version weakened by amendments, so it was sent to a committee composed entirely of members of the joint committee, including Laudadio, Kury, and the joint committee's chair, Republican Representative William Wilt of Blair County, and vice-chair, Democratic Senator Donald Oesterling of Butler County. This bipartisan coalition was made possible by support from rural farming and urban industrial areas, as well as rapidly expanding suburban communities. Protecting water quality thus served as a great unifier for the state's diverse interests. The compromise measure was approved by both houses and sent to Governor Raymond Shafer, who signed it into law on July 31, 1970.[20]

The rapid push of environmental legislation was only possible due to the demands of a broad swath of residents for new laws that went beyond those of the Progressive era. The strong support for public lands funded by Project 70 and Project 500 and the passage of the Pennsylvania Scenic Rivers Act underscored the continuing importance of the preservationist strand of the conservation movement, as well as expanded consumer demand for outdoor recreation. However, the underlying impetus for new environmental regulations was improving the working landscapes residents encountered in their daily lives. The role of chemicals in disrupting the biological systems of plants and animals, as well as humans, was a key theme of *Silent Spring* and built on the work of Pennsylvania-based scientists such as Dr. Ruth Patrick, a pioneering freshwater ecologist at the Academy of Natural Sciences in Philadelphia. This ecological framework underscoring links among humans and the rest of nature made its way into new environmental policies, including a 1968 update to the state's Air Pollution Control Act. The act, with language developed by the joint committee, pushed beyond the original law's relatively modest goal "to maintain such a reasonable degree of purity of the air resources of the Commonwealth as shall be technically feasible, economically reasonable, and necessary for the protection of the normal health" to the more strident demand to "protect the air resources of the Commonwealth to the degree necessary for . . . public health, safety and well-being of its citizens [as well as the] prevention of injury to plant and animal life and property."[21]

The most visible event showing the widespread enthusiasm for this new environmental movement was the first Earth Day in April 1970, conceived by Minnesota Senator Gaylord Nelson as a sit-in modeled on antiwar and civil rights activism. Residents throughout Pennsylvania eagerly embraced Earth Day. Philadelphia's "Earth Week" was the biggest and most publicized of the events, with a crowd of thirty thousand gathered in Fairmount Park to hear the all–Native American rock band Redbone singing their song "Red and Blue" that depicted the "crunch of steel and concrete" as "a beautiful land is dyin'," and the activist Ralph Nader presiding over the signing of the "Declaration of Interdependence" in front of Independence Hall. Many smaller communities also organized events, with classes canceled for the day at Shippensburg State College, for example, and students urged to "Join the Environmental Fight." "The dangers that are threatening our planet are clearly visible," wrote one young activist in the student newspaper, "yet nothing is done to control it." "We must fight pollution," concluded another editorial, "because if this problem goes unsolved, we will not be here to solve any of the other problems."[22]

The environmental protection movement in Pennsylvania also took the form of new advocacy organizations with a more aggressive approach to pollution control. The Group Against Smog and Pollution (GASP) formed in 1969 to protest Pittsburgh's long-standing air quality problems. The founders of GASP saw themselves as a "citizen's action group" and urged fellow residents: "Don't Hold Your Breath! FIGHT FOR IT." Similarly, residents in Delaware County formed the Concerned Area Residents for the Protection of Tinicum Marsh (CARP) in opposition to a proposal to route Interstate 95 through and construct a landfill in the state's largest remaining freshwater tidal wetland; CARP succeeded in securing congressional legislation to protect the area, which became the nation's first urban wildlife refuge. To support efforts such as these, a group of lawyers and environmental professionals, including Joshua Whetzel of the Western Pennsylvania Conservancy and Thomas Dolan IV of the Wissahickon Valley Watershed Association, in the summer of 1969 created the Pennsylvania Environmental Council (PEC) to serve as a statewide "coordinating organization." Immediately, the organization joined the Allegheny Mountain Chapter of Trout Unlimited in a suit against the state and federal governments over plans to reroute a highway in rural Potter County adjacent to Sinnemahoning Creek. While PEC ultimately lost the suit, the decision established the right of a citizens' group to sue the government on matters of broad public concern, which would have far-reaching consequences in the subsequent evolution of U.S. environmental law.[23]

Beyond individual legislative victories in Harrisburg, the most significant public policy shift of the environmental revolution was the creation of the Department of Environmental Resources (DER), a mammoth agency that encompassed the former Department of Forests and Waters and Department of Mines and Mineral Industries, as well as the State Planning Board, and inherited some responsibilities of the departments of Agriculture, Labor and Industry, and Health. The idea for the DER emerged among the legislators and staff of the joint committee who felt that spreading regulatory responsibility across multiple agencies created "a mismatch with the scale of the prob-

Figure 4.3 Governor George Leader signing Water Resources Bill with Dr. Maurice Goddard, secretary of the Department of Forests and Waters, December 15, 1955. (Courtesy: Pennsylvania State Archives, Governor's File, #665, RG-12.)

lems and the reality of the environment's interconnectedness." The text of the bill was primarily developed by Abele, and Laudadio shepherded it through unanimous approval by the House. After some minor modifications by the Senate, Governor Shafer signed it into law on December 3, 1970; a month later, his successor, the Democrat Milton Shapp, retained Maurice Goddard as the new department's secretary (Figure 4.3).[24]

With the revolution in environmental regulation fully underway and the newly integrated DER headed by the state's most respected conservationist, advocates in the legislature turned their attention to permanently enshrining the new ethic of environmentalism in Pennsylvania's foundational document. Intrigued by the addition of a "conservation bill of rights" to New York's constitution, Kury introduced a bill in the House in April 1968 to similarly amend his state's constitution. Following a few minor changes recommended by party leadership and members of the Conservation Committee, the bill cleared the chamber unanimously. With some additional revisions, the Senate, too, voted unanimously to forward the bill, and on April 14, 1970, Kury publicly introduced the concurring resolution on the House floor ahead of a speech by Earth Day's founder, Gaylord Nelson. In January 1971, the proposed amendment was again unanimously passed by both chambers, and in May the state's voters approved it by a four-to-one margin. With the passage of the Environmental Rights Amendment, Pennsylvania's "public natural resources" were declared "the common property of all the people, including generations yet to come." Further, the commonwealth was enjoined as "trustee of these resources" to "conserve and maintain them for the benefit of all the people." Support for environmental protection, with backing from rural, urban, and suburban Pennsylvanians alike, was at its zenith.[25]

Politics of Pollution

About a year after enactment of the Environmental Rights Amendment, Kury joined Goddard at a ceremony to dedicate Shikellamy State Park's new Susquehanna River marina. As Goddard began speaking, it started raining and did not stop for five days. From June 21 through June 24, 1972, Hurricane Agnes, the costliest hurricane ever to hit the state, stalled over Pennsylvania and New York, with much of the region experiencing more than seven inches of precipitation and the western portions of Schuylkill County receiving up to nineteen inches. Some buildings in Harrisburg were under thirteen feet of water as the Susquehanna submerged the first floor of the governor's mansion. Flooding forced more than 100,000 residents to evacuate and destroyed more than sixty-eight thousand homes and three thousand businesses. At least 220,000 people were left homeless, with fifty fatalities and $2.3 billion in losses in Pennsylvania alone.[26]

The enormous damage inflicted by Hurricane Agnes and another major flood in Johnstown later in the decade that killed eighty-five people provided the political urgency to pass new laws in 1978 to comprehensively address stormwater and floodplain management. Indeed, in this and other ways the environmental revolution continued, with nineteen more state parks created between 1972 and 1980, an expanded mandate for protecting water quality and aquatic animals at the Fish Commission, and preserved land by the Game Commission topping more than a million acres. However, the exceptional growth of the postwar period also gave way to a series of economic challenges, including a serious recession from 1973 to 1975 that hit steel-producing areas in Pennsylvania particularly hard. Politicians came under increasing fire from industrialists who, fairly or unfairly, blamed compliance costs of pollution regulations for exacerbating unemployment. Goddard and his staff at the DER were simultaneously criticized by environmental advocates who felt the agency was not moving quickly enough to improve the state's air and water quality. As the decade closed, more and more Pennsylvanians questioned the ability of political leaders to navigate the difficult balance between the consumption and conservation of natural resources.

The incorporation of the Department of Forests and Waters into the new DER signaled the importance of treating the environment as an integrated whole with value beyond that of narrow human economic need. In 1970, the State Forest Commission changed its framework for setting aside scenic areas and adopted a more ecological approach to designating special districts of unique value that should be "maintained in a natural condition by allowing physical and natural processes to operate without direct human intervention." The DER's policy-setting Environmental Quality Board expanded the guidelines for selecting and administering these areas, which grew to thirteen natural and forty-four wild areas covering more than 160,000 acres within state forests. Even as officials struggled to deal with continuing and new threats, such as the defoliation of more than eight million acres of northeastern Pennsylvania forest by spongy moths, department policy emphasized that "State Forest land should provide habitats that support a diversity of animal and plant communities and should serve as examples in promoting the conservation of native wild flora"—a significant shift from monoculture pine plantations of the Progressive era.[27]

Natural resource agencies that remained outside the DER also responded to changing expectations of the environmental revolution. In 1972, Abele was appointed executive director of the Pennsylvania Fish Commission, which historically emphasized raising and stocking waterways with sport fish regardless of broader ecological implications (Figure 4.4). As executive secretary of the joint committee, Abele had helped write many important environmental laws and quickly refocused commission staff on a "Resource First" philosophy that put "protecting, conserving, and enhancing the Commonwealth's aquatic resources [as] the agency's first management priority." Abele devoted numerous "Straight Talk" columns he wrote for the *Pennsylvania Angler* to negative effects of pollution on wildlife habitat and gained a reputation as a fierce fighter against mine drainage, declaring, "If the fish can't survive in the water, there are serious problems for man." The legislature assigned responsibility for protecting reptiles, amphibians, and other aquatic organisms to the commission in 1974 and added penalties for killing endangered species. This shift to treating fish as intrinsic parts of broader environments underscored the impact of ecological thinking on the state's regulatory regime.[28]

This was equally true at the Pennsylvania Game Commission, where funding from Project 70 and Project 500 allowed an expansion to more than

Figure 4.4 Area Fisheries Manager Blake Weirich using a pH kit to test the water in his region, 1986. (Courtesy: Pennsylvania Fish and Boat Commission.)

a million acres of State Game Lands across sixty-five of the sixty-seven counties. This included the spectacular 2,900 acre Middle Creek Wildlife Management Area in Lancaster and Lebanon counties, a vital stopover for snow geese, tundra swans, and other migrating birds. In 1934, the militant conservationist Rosalie Edge had founded the world's first preserve for birds of prey, Hawk Mountain Sanctuary, along the Appalachian flyway west of Allentown. As *Silent Spring* began making household names out of DDT, chlordane, and endrin, the commission joined the crusade to restrict pesticides that, along with overhunting, had virtually eliminated once common bald eagles, peregrine falcons, and other raptors from the state. Continued declines in wildlife populations, often due to habitat loss from suburban sprawl, also led the agency to stop predator bounties on great horned owls and red and gray foxes and, in 1970, to the elimination of hunting bobcats, which had grown scarce throughout most of the state. "Bounties Are Bunk," declared one former commission biologist. "The science of wildlife management has come of age and barbershop biology is rapidly being replaced by true wildlife biology." The commission also adopted the federal endangered species list and later signed a cooperative agreement with the U.S. Fish and Wildlife Service to study and improve the conditions for endangered species, including bald eagles, which were reintroduced to the state beginning in 1979.[29]

Legislative initiatives around environmental protection also continued, though at a slower pace. For Kury, the events of Hurricane Agnes underscored the need for comprehensive stormwater management and planning in floodplains. At the crest of the Agnes flood, the Sunbury *Daily Item* had published a striking photo of the community's flood wall with the Susquehanna River only two inches from the top and an eight-foot drop to Front Street. Kury used this image to emphasize that no amount of flood protection could defend riverine communities from land use decisions made upstream. Fresh off his election to the state senate in 1973, he introduced the Pennsylvania Flood Disaster Prevention Act, cosponsored by three Republicans and three Democrats, including Senate President Martin Murray of Luzerne County, which Agnes had devastated. In effect, the proposed new law mirrored the expansion of state control over sewage treatment and air pollution to encompass land use decisions in flood-prone areas. Kury anticipated that the devastation of Agnes combined with the strong support for environmental legislation in previous legislative sessions would allow for quick passage. He was wrong.[30]

Even by 1973, the tide had begun to turn against further expansion of the environmental revolution. The rise of environmental protection had taken place during an era of unrivaled economic growth and prosperity. The winding down of military-related contracts at the end of the Vietnam War coupled with increasing economic competition from overseas and the continued shift of industrial capacity to other parts of the country placed strains on the state's manufacturing sector. This was exacerbated by a quadrupling of the cost of petroleum following the decision of Arab oil-exporting countries to impose an embargo on the United States in retaliation for aid to Israel in the Yom Kippur War. As a result, arguments for pollution controls, land use planning, and protection of animal habitat that were previously promoted as not requiring burdensome sacrifices now faced stronger pushback from industrialists and their allies who blamed higher production costs due to environmental regulations for unemployment.[31]

Economic recession coupled with higher rates of inflation—the dreaded "stagflation" of the 1970s—also strained state coffers. Political leaders responded by reining in spending, so when Governor Shapp presented his annual budget in May 1973, the $50 million proposed for the DER was well below the department's request. Republicans, who were back in control of the House, further reduced the amount to $48.3 million. The DER's deputy secretary called the budget decision "the most important environmental issue the General Assembly will face this year." Legislators added enormous new responsibilities that ranged from enforcing air pollution, clean streams, strip mining, and snowmobile permitting to developing a statewide environmental master plan, he continued, "without any new money to implement them." Leonard Green, chairman of the DER's Citizens' Advisory Council, reported that Secretary Goddard told him that budget cuts might mean that two new Philadelphia-area parks and additions to four others could not be opened. "DER is responsible for the air we breathe, the water we drink, swim and fish in, sewage disposal, parks, mines, energy and job safety," Green concluded. "The environment is going to be hurt damned bad because of this."[32]

Goddard had eventually agreed to serve as DER secretary, but he publicly opposed the consolidation of the Department of Forests and Waters into a new "environmental superagency" that, he felt, uneasily combined regulatory and conservation responsibilities and ran the risk of becoming overly politicized. The budget debate demonstrated that Goddard was right to be concerned. As environmental regulations proliferated at both the state and federal level, the DER required a rapidly expanding cadre of lawyers, engineers, and field inspectors, as well as expensive monitoring equipment, to handle complex legal and technical issues. With political leaders unwilling to increase agency budgets to keep up with growing needs, this often meant resources had to be shifted away from maintaining state parks and forests even as public demand increased. The environmental revolution's bipartisan consensus also quickly gave way to criticism of pollution enforcement measures, especially among Republicans, who sensed a way to peel working-class support away from Democrats. In neighboring Ohio, for example, the Republican James Rhodes roared back into office for a third term as governor in 1978 declaring, "We're not going to roll over and play dead" and casting himself as a defender of industrial and mining jobs against "E[nvironmental] P[rotection] A[gency] mandates that are forcing Ohio mines to close."[33]

William Eichbaum, the DER's deputy secretary for enforcement, became the lightning rod for antienvironmental sentiment in Pennsylvania. In the summer of 1970, the Shafer administration tapped Eichbaum, a Philadelphia attorney who been part of a lawsuit to preserve Tinicum Marsh, to help address concerns that state agencies were not effectively enforcing new regulations. State judges were initially reluctant to apply the new and relatively unfamiliar body of environmental law, but soon the DER's "environmental strike force" launched dozens of high-profile enforcement actions against industrial polluters. In 1972, for example, senior executives at U.S. Steel, Bethlehem Steel, and Jones and Laughlin were invited to Harrisburg to discuss draft regulations for coal coking ovens. When confronted with the proposals' scale and scope, Eichbaum recalled, "the shock and indignation of the industry representatives was extreme." It took a consent decree in 1976 to finally force coke oven operators into compliance with air pollution laws, and that was not until after U.S. Steel commissioned a series of full-page newspaper ads questioning whether it should have built their new headquarters in Pittsburgh in the face of such aggressive enforcement. These environmentalists have "practically destroyed their credibility . . . with their irresponsible statements," complained one letter to the Pittsburgh *Post-Gazette*; their board meetings should always "include at least two persons who are unemployed steelworkers. Perhaps then their judgements will be tempered by the reason necessary."[34]

Regulations became such a fraught political subject that even Representative Laudadio and Senator Kury—the two politicians most associated with the state's environmental revolution—found themselves under pressure from constituents to intervene in the DER's activities. In 1975, over Eichbaum's objection, Kury prevailed on Goddard to reverse DER staff's determination that a proposed new highway in his district was impossible to build without adverse environmental impacts. The next year, amid high-profile enforcement efforts against big steel companies, Laudadio, a retired Westinghouse engineer whose Pittsburgh-area district was heavily industrialized, proposed transferring enforcement responsibility out of the DER and publicly suggested that Goddard had "lost control over the strike force lawyers." "The department has a serious public image problem," he declared, "and I'm sure the 253 members of the General Assembly are aware of this, based on the complaints they get from their constituents." In the end, it took extensive lobbying from environmental groups and Goddard's threat to resign for Laudadio to back down.[35]

Even as they came under fire for aggressive enforcement of pollution regulations, Goddard and his staff faced pressure from citizen activists who felt they too often privileged consumption over conservation of natural resources. Indeed, the secretary's confirmation had been held up for six months by Senator Edwin Holl, who opposed a proposed dam at Evansburg State Park in Montgomery County. Holl slammed "Goddard's approach to environmental problems [as] hopelessly outdated," a view shared by the Pennsylvania chapter of the Sierra Club, which suggested that Goddard's record did "not hold promise for the kind of leadership, imagination, and concern" needed for the new department. The issue of dam construction proved especially troublesome to the secretary throughout his tenure. Among these was the Kinzua Dam on the Allegheny River, a flood control project designed to protect downstream communities, especially Pittsburgh, that came at the expense of approximately six hundred Seneca residents forced to relocate from land originally granted by treaty to Chief Cornplanter in 1794. While the project was federal, Goddard offered his full-throated endorsement, declaring that, while it was "unfortunate that any citizen, no matter what his origin, must give up his beloved home for an urgently needed public project," he was "certain that in the final analysis the Senecas w[ould] see the necessity for this project, which most economically meets the needs of their fellow Americans downstream." Instead, "Remember Kinzua" became a rallying cry for proponents of Native American rights.[36]

The Evansburg dam proposal slammed during Goddard's confirmation hearing in 1971 was part of a broader scheme to provide flood control and drinking water centered on a large Delaware River dam at Tocks Island. For Goddard, who strongly supported the project, the case was clear to serve the needs of "the average citizen of the Basin who . . . won't be heard from until he is flooded [or] until his tap runs dry." But for the Sierra Club, Save the Delaware River Coalition, and other opponents, the proposal would have created a thirty-seven-mile environmental disaster "like Vietnam," in the words of a biologist at East Stroudsburg State College. In 1975, the Delaware River Basin Commission, over the objection of Governor Shapp, finally voted to shelve the Tocks Island project, with the land already acquired incorporated into the Delaware Water Gap National Recreation Area. Ultimately, the Tocks Island proposal became a casualty of ballooning cost estimates as the federal government cut domestic spending amid the war in Vietnam, but clearly by this point any consensus regarding the proper balance between consumption and conservation of Pennsylvania's natural resources had evaporated.[37]

In the end, Pennsylvania's environmental revolution carried through to the enactment of comprehensive floodplain control legislation that Kury had first proposed in the wake of Hurricane Agnes. However, the changing political dynamics of the 1970s meant that it took five years and became the "most contentious and fiercely contested issue of [his] legislative experience." As difficult as it was to regulate industrial polluters, Kury later reflected that he "failed to appreciate [the] emotional opposition that would arise because of the traditional resentment of state government regulations by local governments," as well as citizens who "resented the seeming avalanche of pesky regulations that now befell them from the Department of Environmental Resources." *Silent Spring* may have alerted Pennsylvanians to the dangers of

pollution, and yet another major Johnstown flood underscored the folly of ig-
noring environmental limits, but "property owners who believed they should
be allowed to build without more government interference" helped fuel growing sentiment that government bureaucrats could not be trusted to manage
the natural world. Instead, a resurgence in conservative politics advocated a
more voluntarist approach that emphasized public-private partnerships and
limiting environmental regulations that might undercut economic growth.[38]

5

POSTINDUSTRIAL PENNSYLVANIA

A S HE PICKED UP THE TELEPHONE just before 8:00 on the morning of March 28, 1979, Governor Dick Thornburgh had no idea the call would help define his legacy and change the course of history. There had been an accident at the Three Mile Island nuclear power plant, located on the Susquehanna River just ten miles downstream from Harrisburg (Figure 5.1). Soon the initials "TMI" would become a stand-in for nuclear energy's dangers, as a simple stuck cooling-system valve eventually resulted in one of the site's two reactors overheating and the worst commercial nuclear power accident in U.S. history. Amid confusion that ensued over the following five days, pregnant women and children were advised to evacuate the area and nearby schools were closed, even as the plant's operator, Metropolitan Edison, along with state and federal officials emphasized the relatively small amounts of radiation escaping from the facility.[1]

The accident at TMI had wide consequences as activists stressed the dangers of nuclear power just as trust in scientists, industrial corporations, and government officials was waning. Soon, Ronald Reagan would declare during his presidential inauguration that "government is not the solution to our problem, government is the problem"; clearly the era of expanding environmental protections was over. Rather than more regulation and public land purchases, Pennsylvanians during the 1980s and 1990s developed new tools for voluntary preservation of abandoned railroad lines, historic sites, and farmland. Residents reimagined shuttered factories as vibrant sites for economic development even as the regulatory reforms of the environmental rev-

Figure 5.1 Aerial view of Middletown, Pennsylvania, and suburbs, with the Three Mile Island nuclear plant in background, September 12, 1979. (Courtesy: Library of Congress, *U.S. News & World Report* Collection.)

olution resulted in clearer air, cleaner water, and the resurgence of wildlife. In practice, this often meant using the remnants of working landscapes that no longer served their original purpose to evoke nostalgic impressions of the industrial past and draw in visitors.[2]

As the twenty-first century dawned, competing ethics of consumption and conservation continued to fuel political tensions, particularly as the discovery of an enormous reserve of natural gas brought with it both economic opportunities and environmental threats. As in the past, environmental amenities were distributed unevenly, with the benefits often going to middle- and upper-class White people, while the poor and people of color were forced to fight for their rights to a healthy environment. However, federal and state agencies also began to take seriously the issue of environmental justice as residents challenged the placement of polluting industries in poor and often minority neighborhoods. Finally, increasingly apparent impacts of global climate change added new urgency to confronting these thorny questions, though it remains unclear whether Pennsylvania's rural, urban, and suburban communities will be able to muster the same level of consensus that allowed past generations to address pressing environmental problems.

The Nature of Deindustrialization

The term *deindustrialization* broadly refers to the relative decline of manufacturing employment in the world's most advanced economies in the late twentieth century. The steel industry in southwestern Pennsylvania, once the planet's greatest industrial conglomeration, collapsed so spectacularly that by 1988 manufacturing accounted for only 14 percent of Pittsburgh's workforce, compared with about 20 percent statewide. Growth in other sectors was not sufficient to compensate for these rapid losses, and as unemployment fueled outmigration, Pennsylvania's overall population declined between 1972 and 1984 and did not begin to rebound for nearly a decade. "Pittsburgh looks beautiful," declared Lane Kirkland, president of the American Federation of Labor-Congress of Industrial Organizations (AFL-CIO), on a visit in 1985 to the Monongahela River Valley, where the number of steelworkers had plummeted from more than thirty-five thousand to fewer than four thousand in just six years. "But I'd like to see it a little dirtier, a little more smoke. The most environmentally offensive thing I see is the shutdown mills."[3]

As Kirkland's remarks suggest, the conservative resurgence marked by the election of Ronald Reagan as president in 1980 brought a policy agenda that, in part, blamed environmentalism for the economic disruptions of deindustrialization. In a campaign visit to the Ohio Valley, for example, Reagan linked job losses in the steel industry to overly burdensome regulations. "Rather than reduce the intrusion of government into our lives," he declared, the Carter administration had "put in place a group of no-growth advocates in Washington." In Pennsylvania, Thornburgh, a Republican who served as governor from 1979 to 1987, similarly declared his opposition to "high taxes, excessive regulatory burdens . . . , and a generally antibusiness mentality in the bureaucracy" but remained more supportive of environmental protection than others in his party. While Thornburgh later took pride in cutting "nearly 15,000 unnecessary positions" from state government, for instance, he highlighted an increased number of Department of Environmental Resources (DER) personnel during his time in office. The governor signed significant new laws dealing with solid waste disposal, energy conservation, and drinking water protection, along with strengthening surface mining and drilling regulations. Indeed, in recognition of his leadership on environmental issues, the Pennsylvania Fish and Game Protection Association awarded Thornburgh its Gold Medal in 1982, the same award it had given Gifford Pinchot fifty years earlier.[4]

Scandal plagued the outgoing administration of Governor Milton Shapp, and Thornburgh made clear his "sweeping mandate to clean out Harrisburg." While he was not involved in any of the wrongdoing, this meant the end of Maurice Goddard's long government career. His replacement as DER secretary, Clifford Jones, was highly regarded as a competent administrator and generally continued Goddard's policies, though he lacked a forestry background. However, concerns about government bureaucracy and regulation dovetailed with a significant budget deficit to end public land expansion. Between 1960 and 1979, Pennsylvania had added thirty-five new parks; that number dropped to seven between 1980 and 1999. Nevertheless, visitation continued to grow so much that by 1987 state parks had an economic impact of $562 million and supported ten thousand jobs. Consequently, attention shifted to the enormous responsibility of maintaining park facilities during a time of fiscal austerity. In recognition of the magnitude of this task, as well as the continued popularity of public lands, the Keystone Recreation, Park and Conservation Fund (Key 93) won overwhelming support in 1993 in both the legislature and a public referendum, authorizing a $50 million bond for deferred maintenance at state parks and historic sites.[5]

As existing antipollution regulations and land use controls slowly improved working landscapes, conservation programs reintroduced wildlife species to the state's rivers and skies. Ralph Abele's leadership at the Pennsylvania

Figure 5.2 Fledgling bald eagle from the Pennsylvania Game Commission's reintroduction program, ca. 1985. (Courtesy: Charles Campfield, Pennsylvania Game Commission.)

Fish Commission led to the construction of an elaborate fish ladder on the Conowingo Dam that allowed shad to return to the mid-Susquehanna River in 1972.[6] Soon afterward, the Delaware River Shad Fisherman's Association began a campaign to get the fish restored to the Lehigh River, which eventually resulted in a $3.3 million state appropriation to build fishways on two other dams. The opening of these structures in 1995 allowed a once ubiquitous species to return for the first time in more than 150 years. Similarly, between 1983 and 1989, the Pennsylvania Game Commission launched a program to raise and release eaglets from Saskatchewan (Figure 5.2). In 1988, a bald eagle nest was found in Tioga County's Pine Creek Gorge, believed to be the first established in eastern Pennsylvania in decades. A year later, five eaglets fledged from eight Pennsylvania nests, including pairs spotted in Dauphin, Lancaster, and York counties.[7]

As sentiment shifted away from increased regulation and public land purchases as preferred conservation methods, Pennsylvanians also pioneered new tools for voluntary preservation of farmland. In 1980, county commissioners in Lancaster County created the state's first Agricultural Preserve Board, which used tax revenues to purchase development rights and maintain private properties as working farms rather than suburban housing tracts or shopping malls. Balancing respect for private property rights while working toward a public good, the program proved incredibly popular and in 1988 voters approved a $100 million bond program to fund agricultural preservation statewide. Over the next thirty years, Pennsylvania led the nation in farmland preservation, with more than 550,000 acres and more than 5,300 farms preserved at a cost of more than $1.5 billion.[8]

Investment in state parks, wildlife protection, and farmland preservation demonstrated continuing public support for conservation, but dealing with environmental pollution proved more difficult, especially as the most egregious examples faded from public memory. A 1983 study analyzing the Chesapeake Bay's continuing loss of aquatic organisms and wildlife pointed to excess nutrient pollution, primarily from insufficiently treated sewage and runoff from farms in the Susquehanna River, the bay's largest freshwater source. Over the previous five years, state and federal agencies had provided more than $250 million for the construction of sewage facilities in the bay's watershed, but dealing with agricultural sources proved more intractable. Farmers often had less ability to control runoff and had always assumed streams could dilute any animal or fertilizer wastes. Lancaster County, which contains only 1.5 percent of the watershed's landmass, for example, produced seventy-two million pounds of nitrogen from animal manure, about 12 percent of the total. In June 1983, Governor Thornburgh hosted his counterparts from Maryland and Virginia, along with the federal Environmental Protection Agency administrator, at a summit that, with the subsequent addition of the District of Columbia, led to the creation of the Chesapeake Bay Commission. "The Chesapeake is one of our most precious, and most fragile national treasures," Thornburgh declared. "This agreement recognizes that any successful effort to restore and protect the bay must reach beyond state boundaries."[9]

Achieving meaningful reduction in agricultural runoff, however, required the enactment of new regulations often seen as intruding into private aspects of farm management. In 1987, Pennsylvania agreed to a 40 percent reduction in nutrient pollution, an effort designed to stave off direct federal oversight under the Clean Water Act. It then took until 1992 to forge compromise legislation that was acceptable to the Pennsylvania Farm Bureau and most other farm groups, as well as to environmental advocates, including the Sierra Club and the Chesapeake Bay Foundation. In return for implementing nutrient management plans, farm operations that produced large amounts of manure could receive grants that defrayed the costs of mitigation projects and protection from potential penalties. The requirements applied only to relatively large producers, meaning that participation for most farmers was voluntary. However, even this modest measure died in the legislature after a coalition that called itself the Family Farm Movement disrupted Senate hearings. This is "the most important piece of legislation to come before this committee while I've been chairman," declared Senator Edward Helfrick. "I think 99 percent of the farmers here today do not support this legislation." While the Pennsylvania Nutrient Management Act did eventually become law, implementation took until 1997, and annual appropriations to assist farmers in managing runoff remained chronically short of meeting the actual needs.[10]

This difficulty in finding workable political compromises between natural resource consumption and conservation in Pennsylvania's waterways was mirrored in the skies. As the danger of potential meltdown and questions about storing radioactive waste haunted the nuclear industry after TMI, mining companies and their allies increasingly cast coal as the responsible solution to the nation's energy needs. Governor Thornburgh "made coal development a major priority," and the state spent $23.6 million to enlarge and modernize coal export facilities in Philadelphia, as well as millions more on upgrades to transportation infrastructure. "I believe that Pennsylvania can and should become the energy capital of the northeast," he declared in 1980. Coal-fired electrical generation faced headwinds, however, from federal environmental regulations, beginning with the passage of the Clean Air Act (CAA) in 1970. Seeking to meet ambient air quality standards in the cheapest way possible, many power plant operators simply built taller exhaust chimneys to disperse pollutants over a broader area. Indeed, when Indiana County's Homer City Generating Station brought its Unit 3 online in 1977, its exhaust chimney was just a little shorter than the Empire State Building.[11]

While chimney height brought power plants into technical CAA compliance, they created a new problem that ultimately provoked an interstate and international crisis. Bituminous coal mined in northern Appalachia has a high proportion of dissolved sulfur, which had long caused water pollution from acid mine drainage. After being released during burning, this same sulfur flowed into the upper atmosphere through tall chimneys and combined with water molecules to produce acidic rain that fell to Earth often hundreds of miles away. As both recipients of acid rain from midwestern emitters and significant producers of coal, Pennsylvanians were deeply divided over dealing with the issue. A 1984 study found that acid rain wiped out the trout population in thirteen of sixty-one streams examined in the Laurel Highlands east of Pittsburgh. Despite increasing evidence, however, a competing report issued by the Pennsylvania Coal Mining Association dismissed claims of environmental damage, declaring, "No one, including the environmentalists, knows the absolute cause and effect relationship of acid rain."[12]

Amid these continued tensions that seemed to pit concerns about the environment and public health against threats of job losses and higher utility rates, both Thornburgh and his successor, Democratic Governor Bob Casey, embraced so-called clean coal technologies that promised to remove sulfur from emissions. As with the agricultural runoff polluting the Chesapeake Bay, this increasingly put Pennsylvania's political leaders from both parties at odds with environmental groups, such as the Sierra Club, who called on Casey to "work to solve the acid rain crisis, not just point the finger at other states upwind from Pennsylvania." Acid rain was finally tackled on a national level through amendments to the CAA in 1991 that established an emissions trading system—just the type of "market incentives" favored by conservatives. Indeed, after leaving the Governor's Office, Thornburgh served as attorney-general under President Reagan and then George H. W. Bush, a role that made him the nation's top enforcer of environmental law. "We count on this market approach to achieve significant reductions in acid rain," Thornburgh declared in 1991, "at a far cheaper rate, and without sole resort to sanctions."[13]

Recycling Pennsylvania's Treasures

When Thomas Murphy was young, his mother warned against going down to Pittsburgh's dirty rivers. After becoming mayor in 1994, Murphy made riverfront revitalization central to his administration, including the conversion of abandoned rail lines into biking and pedestrian trails. "Early in our history the rivers defined who we are," Murphy wrote. "But, for the last hundred years the rivers served only the industry of Pittsburgh. . . . The railroads took the best properties, flat scenic land along the rivers. Those lands are becoming available now, and we need to take the opportunity to use them." By 1999, as the region's economy struggled to move past the shock of deindustrialization, Pittsburgh was so successful in recycling abandoned riverfronts and rail lines that it was selected to host the second International Greenways and Rails-to-Trails Conference. "It's bittersweet to see our industry gone and things change, but Pittsburgh has been on the world's center stage twice, during the French and Indian War and the Industrial Revolution," Murphy concluded. "We have a wonderful story to tell about the city's past and want to make that history part of our city's future."[14]

Within a context of decreased funding and increased skepticism of government, many Pennsylvanians worked to craft public-private partnerships to

Figure 5.3 New Jersey Zinc Company, Palmerton Plant, Carbon County, Pennsylvania. Placed on the Superfund program's National Priorities List in 1983. (Courtesy: Library of Congress, Historic American Engineering Record.)

remake the state's working landscapes. Among the most pressing issues was what to do with the thousands of abandoned industrial sites known as brown-fields, blighted residential properties, and declining commercial districts scat-tered throughout Pennsylvania's communities. Following high-profile inci-dents of hazardous wastes making their way into human activities—most notably, at Love Canal in Niagara Falls, New York—the federal government passed the Comprehensive Environmental Response, Compensation and Lia-bility Act (Superfund), which taxed oil and chemical companies to provide funding to identify and remediate hazardous waste sites (Figure 5.3). The government could sue responsible parties to pay for cleanup, as it did in the case of Publicker Industries when a multi-alarm fire in 1987 revealed 850,000 gallons of alcohol, antifreeze, cleansers, and PCB-contaminated oil at an abandoned thirty-seven-acre site in Philadelphia. The hazards at the facility, which had previously made Old Hickory bourbon and industrial alcohol, were so notorious that Governor Casey used it as the backdrop to announce plans for a state version of Superfund, which he signed into law in 1988.[15]

Pennsylvania was among the first states to develop effective policies for the daunting task of remediating these types of former industrial sites. In many locations it was difficult even to figure out what hazardous materials might be on a property, a problem that made working with brownfields both expensive and time-consuming. For example, developers on a state-subsidized project to remake the former site of Jones and Laughlin Steel into the Pittsburgh Technology Center began work in 1983 before unexpectedly finding toxic ferrous cyanide from a coal tar storage tank used by the Consolidated Gas Company more than sixty years before. This single oversight caused a two-year delay as engineers struggled to devise a suitable mitigation strategy. In the end, one of the site's tenants, Carnegie Mellon University, had to relocate its Research Institute away from the hazardous material, and another portion of the site could not be developed at all. Experiences such as this convinced the General Assembly to pass legislation in 1995 creating uniform standards for remediation, financing options for brownfield locations, and liability releases for approved cleanups. Over the next twenty-five years, this Land Recycling Program expanded to more than six thousand sites and became a national model.[16]

Still, brownfield redevelopment remained a very difficult process, especially in small communities with few financial resources. In Duquesne and McKeesport, for example, a developer removed 2,200 barrels of oil chemicals and other toxic liquids, disposed of asbestos-lined pipes and tanks, eliminated old PCB-laden electrical transformers, and even dug up an old railcar from two former steel mill sites. In tiny Taylor Borough, just outside Scranton, the 150-acre Taylor Colliery shut down in the 1960s, but it was not until 2003 that local leaders secured the first of a series of brownfield recovery grants to begin salvaging the property. It then took until 2010 for the state's Bureau of Abandoned Mine Land Reclamation to complete a $1.4 million remediation of eighty-five acres that eliminated such environmental hazards as mine spoil piles and embankments, vertical mine shafts, abandoned equipment, and structural debris. Still, as late as 2018 the site remained unoccupied. "We have invested probably close to $3 million in upgrading the property. It still needs some work out there," opined one local official. "Despite all the rumors going around, there is nobody that has stepped forward. Nobody is looking to buy it yet. Hopefully, somebody will."[17]

Even when pollution was not a significant factor, landowners and communities regularly struggled to adapt the historical built environment for contemporary needs. Urban renewal had often emphasized razing infrastructure and starting anew, which could tear apart the very communities that officials sought to help. Instead, a coalition of historic preservationists, urban planners, and community activists advocated updating and reusing existing buildings. This "blending of the old and the new" found its first expression in the late 1960s in the efforts of the Pittsburgh History and Landmarks Foundation (PHLF) to redevelop residential neighborhoods on that city's North Side. In 1970, the National Trust for Historic Places declared Pittsburgh "a preservation laboratory" that avoided "shunt[ing] off the poor to faceless projects." The PHLF later helped launch the city's Renaissance II initiative by transforming the abandoned Pittsburgh and Lake Erie Railroad terminal into Station Square, a fifty-two-acre mixed-use commercial site. In the 1980s, Philadelphia, too, began embracing adaptive reuse as the for-profit Historic Landmarks for Living converted several Old City factories and other abandoned industrial buildings into apartments that helped reimagine the downtown. "Hopefully this will keep going until we remove all the blight from Philadelphia," declared one development official. "It takes hundreds of developers to do that, so everyone's got to get on board."[18]

Rural residents, too, struggled to adapt working landscapes for contemporary needs, including the rail corridors that were once the lifeblood of thousands of small communities. Often this meant turning former places of industrial production into sites of recreational consumption. Six thousand miles of railroad had been abandoned in Pennsylvania by the time Thomas Murphy, who served as a legislator before being elected Pittsburgh mayor, shepherded a bill through the General Assembly in 1990 authorizing the state to "acquire and develop available railroad rights-of-way for public recreational trail use." While a few properties were directly acquired by the state or part of state-owned sites, usually local governments and not-for-profit trail groups sponsored and maintained rail trails, with a portion of their funding provided by state grants. "People will come from all over the country, all over the world to use those kinds of trails," Murphy declared at the time, and he was right. The most significant early trail to be completed under the new program was the sixty-two-mile Pine Creek Rail Trail in Lycoming and Tioga counties, which opened its first section in 1996. Within a decade, the trail had received an estimated 125,000 visits annually, and an article in *USA Today* named the route one of "10 Great Places to Take a Bike Tour."[19]

In an era of decreased public spending and government intervention, promoters touted rail trails as tools for community development, outdoor recreation, heritage promotion, and environmental protection. As with other adaptive reuses of brownfield sites, however, trail development was often a complicated process requiring significant economic and political capital as well as sustainable public-private partnerships. For example, both state and federal officials had turned down an offer from the Western Maryland Railway in 1975 to acquire its route between Cumberland, Maryland, and Connellsville for use as a linear park due to concerns about the potential costs, maintenance, and difficulty in administration. Unable to broker a deal for the full route, the Western Pennsylvania Conservancy in June 1978 purchased and transferred to the state fifteen miles of right-of-way within and just outside the boundaries of Ohiopyle State Park. The first nine miles of trail opened in 1986 and proved incredibly popular with park visitors. Nearby communities took note and completed the 150 mile route, known as the Great Allegheny Passage, that extended from Point State Park in Pittsburgh to the Chesapeake and Ohio Canal National Historical Park in Cumberland. While the Great Allegheny Passage eventually proved a success, it took more than thirty years to build, requiring long-term commitments from a coalition of business boosters, cycling enthusiasts, civic leaders, and environmentalists, who formed a handful of not-for-profit trail groups, as well as millions of dollars in funding from the local, state, and federal government.[20]

Beyond tensions between consumption and conservation of resources, campaigners struggled with protecting built and natural environments while ensuring their efforts improved quality of life for all residents. As Arthur Ziegler, who cofounded the PHLF, once declared, "Our primary goal is not preservation as an end in itself. [Rather,] preservation is a tool for achieving economic vitality and a better quality of life for our citizens." The expansion of environmental regulations provided opportunities for citizens to weigh in on whether polluting industries were appropriate for sites, for example, but the way those debates played out tended to break down along race and class lines. During the industrial era, there was often a tacit agreement that a paycheck was available for those willing to work in hazardous environments. With employees' homes generally located near sites of production, workers' families, too, were exposed to smoke and other pollution. As deindustrialization left many residents in need of jobs and poor communities desperate for tax revenues, local officials increasingly sought out polluting industries, such as waste incinerators and garbage dumps, as the best solution available to them. Further, the difficulty in transforming brownfields to other uses meant that these locations were often seen as being most suitable for continued polluting use, even by regulators. As a result, the mainstream environmental movement became associated with NIMBY-ism (Not in My Backyard) and was critiqued by those advocating a more socially just approach to environmental issues.[21]

A key example of this emerging environmental justice movement developed in the Delaware County community of Chester. Deindustrialization hit

Chester hard as its median family income and population dropped by nearly half between 1970 and 2010, while the percentage of Black and Hispanic residents grew to more than 80 percent. At the same time, a proposal to build a large waste incinerator at South Philadelphia's abandoned Naval Yard stalled in the face of local opposition. Instead, massive local unemployment and a dearth of tax revenues in Chester prompted Mayor Willie Mae Leake to suggest siting a facility in her city's brownfields along the Delaware River. County commissioners subsequently expanded the incinerator's size and diverted much of the operating profit to county coffers, even though Chester residents were the ones directly suffering the degraded environment. When the Delaware Valley Resource Recovery Facility (DVRRF) opened in 1991, it received trash from as far away as New York City and was one of the largest incinerators in the nation, with a daily burning capacity of more than 3,500 tons.[22]

The factors that made Chester's waterfront a viable location for the DVRRF were then used to justify the siting of similarly noxious facilities nearby, including an infectious waste sterilization plant, a contaminated soil remediation facility, and a sewage treatment plant. As a result, a 1995 study concluded that "both cancer and non-cancer risks . . . from the pollution sources at locations in the city of Chester exceed levels which [the Environmental Protection Agency] believes are acceptable." By that point, Chester residents, including Horace Strand, pastor of Faith Temple Holy Church, and Zulene Mayfield formed Chester Residents Concerned for Quality Living (CRCQL) to advocate for a better living environment. In 1996, CRCQL filed a first-of-its-kind complaint in federal court accusing state regulators of creating a "discriminatory effect" by allowing the clustering of waste facilities in Chester. While the suit was ultimately declared moot by the U.S. Supreme Court, it established a principle that citizens could sue over issues of environmental justice; in 2004, Pennsylvania regulators initiated a policy that expanded public input for permitting in communities with a high percentage of minority residents or poverty-level incomes. "There are a lot of people cheering for Chester right now because they're living the same lives," declared Dr. Robert Bullard, a sociologist who is widely considered the father of the environmental justice movement. "People have the right to exercise their constitutional right for fairness and equal treatment."[23]

Living Landscapes

The two hundred acre parcel that George Lambert bought in the early 1930s was typical for the rugged Laurel Highlands in Somerset County. He timbered it to generate income during the Great Depression and later sold lots for hunting cabins. Neighboring properties were strip mined, but the Lambert land had no coal of sufficient value, and George's grandson, Tim, who inherited the property in the 1990s, remembered it primarily as a place he spent childhood days picking blackberries and fishing. That all changed on September 11, 2001, when passengers of United Airlines Flight 93 revolted against hijackers who intended to fly into the U.S. Capitol and during the struggle crashed the plane into the Lambert property, with no survivors. Over the next decade, the U.S. National Park Service (NPS) acquired part of Lambert's land and that of his neighbors to create a national memorial for the victims of Flight 93. "I think because it was in sort of the nation's heartland, in a rural part of Pennsylvania, people go there and use their visit as a time to reflect," Lambert explained. "And it gives them a chance to just kind of be in the moment and enjoy the peacefulness, the solitude, nature regenerating over the years."[24]

The transformation of the Lambert property into the Flight 93 National Memorial is a particularly poignant example of shifting and often complicated relationships between conservation and consumption in twenty-first-century working landscapes. The establishment of the Gettysburg Battlefield Memorial Association in 1864 shows the commonwealth's long history of preserving culturally significant landscapes. The site of the Continental Army's encampment at Valley Forge became Pennsylvania's first state park in 1893, the same year that the Forestry Commission was created.[25] Other state parks also came to encompass culturally significant sites, such as Pine Grove Furnace in Cumberland County, but it was not until public interest surrounding the American Bicentennial that officials began thinking seriously about a heritage parks program. In May 1978, Jerry Wettstone, inaugural director of the Bureau of Recreation and Conservation in the Department of Community Affairs, sent a letter inviting colleagues to a presentation on New York State's proposed urban cultural park system. "I've become increasingly interested," Wettstone wrote, "in the relationship between historic preservation, urban cultural parks and neighborhood preservation." Deindustrialization added additional impetus, and by 1987 the heritage areas concept was linked to a "framework for public/private partnerships essential for community and economic revitalization." Finally in 1989, the legislature provided funding to support eight heritage parks: Lackawanna Valley, Allegheny Ridge, Delaware and Lehigh Canal, Schuylkill River, Oil Region, National Road, Rivers of Steel (Mon Valley), and the Lumber Region.[26]

As state heritage areas began to take shape alongside a similar NPS initiative, Goddard's long-standing campaign to split the Department of Environmental Resources into two agencies finally came to fruition shortly before his death in 1995 with the support of Republican Governor Tom Ridge. The first secretary of the new Department of Conservation and Natural Resources (DCNR), John C. Oliver, emphasized "a brighter future for Pennsylvania's natural resources" that would be managed under the principles of *"steward-ship, partnership, and service."* In addition to overseeing the state's forests and parks, DCNR acquired the Bureau of Recreation and Conservation, including Heritage Areas, and its emphasis on fostering local economic development through public-private partnerships among individuals, businesses, municipalities, the federal government, and other state agencies. In practice, this often meant using the remnants of working landscapes that no longer served their original purpose to evoke nostalgic impressions of the industrial or agricultural past. "Let's use these old industries to bring economic rejuvenation to this area," explained the president of the Susquehanna Gateway Heritage Area, established in 2001. "We can make an industry of it."[27]

Tourism development was a key driver of heritage areas, but state officials and local partners framed their broader mission in the same terms as preservationists who sought to instill a strong sense of place among residents of urban historic districts. "Now we would say we're focusing on important Pennsylvania stories," explained Brenda Barrett, who served as the coordinator of heritage areas at the NPS before she joined the DCNR as director of the Bureau of Recreation and Conservation. "This is different from tourism. It's about local identity." By 2004, the Heritage Areas program had laid the foundation for a broader shift as the DCNR launched what would become the Conservation Landscapes Initiative (CLI), which would encompass both "built assets and communities" and "natural resources and ecosystems . . . on a landscape scale." The initial seven CLIs (an eighth was later added) varied in both size, from the sprawling "Pennsylvania Wilds" to the more modest "Susquehanna Riverlands," and focus, but in broad terms rapid urban encroachment in the eastern half of the state placed a priority on land conservation, trails, and recreational development. In the north and west, deindustrialization, population declines, and environmental remediation of mine drainage meant that "desired outcomes" initially focused primarily on "community revitalization and tourism."[28]

The same year that the DCNR launched the CLI, Texas-based Range Resources began testing the possibility of combining two drilling technologies—hydraulic fracturing and horizontal drilling—to extract natural gas from a previously untapped rock structure known as the Marcellus Shale. Success at the company's first drill site in Washington County led to purchasing additional acreage and perfecting its technique to such an extent that it expanded from fewer than one hundred million cubic feet of natural gas per day in 2009 to two hundred million in 2010, five hundred million in 2012, and an average daily production of two billion cubic feet equivalent in 2017. By 2015, there were more than seventy thousand active gas wells in the state, placing it second only to Texas, and energy executives were referring to Pennsylvania as "the Saudi Arabia of natural gas."[29]

As drilling and pipeline companies, support industries, and workers flooded into the western and northern counties that overlay gas-bearing shales, this revolution in "fracking," as the extraction process became known, added a new layer to working landscapes and raised new questions about the appropriate use of natural resources. Royalty checks from gas drillers provided a lucrative lifeline to supplement struggling farms, while other residents saw opportunities for jobs in the gas industry to make up for steep declines in coal mining and manufacturing. Local and state governments expected windfalls from expanded property and income taxes, while officials across the political spectrum trumpeted Pennsylvania's ability to attract energy-intensive industries, including refineries to create plastics and other petroleum-based products. In 2016, for example, Shell announced its decision to build a major petrochemical plant along the Ohio River in Beaver County that would use shale gas to produce 1.6 million tons of polyethylene each year. With "Shell's investment in the region," declared one official, "we'll be primed in a way we could not have previously imagined to further grow an industry—petrochemicals—that already has a foothold here."[30]

For others, the term *fracking* connoted the latest phase in a long history of profiting from natural resource exploitation at the expense of public health and the environment. The burning of natural gas produced fewer direct emissions than coal, but advocates for wind, solar, and nuclear energy pointed out that these methods caused no air pollution at all. The migration of methane and chemicals from the drilling process away from well sites also provoked fears of groundwater contamination that captured public attention through films such as the Emmy Award–winning documentary *Gasland* (2010) and Eliza Griswold's Pulitzer Prize–winning book, *Amity and Prosperity: One Family and the Fracturing of America*. Political wrangling over how best to manage benefits and costs from natural gas extraction resulted in the passage of Act 13 in 2012, which imposed a modest impact fee on new wells but also limited the ability of local governments to place zoning and other restrictions on shale gas wells. Over the next decade, the Republican-dominated legislature also diverted oil and gas royalties from state lands that had traditionally gone to support conservation efforts into the general fund and defeated proposals to add taxes on natural gas extraction.[31]

Figure 5.4 Wind turbines, Somerset County, ca. 2005. (Courtesy: The State Museum of Pennsylvania.)

Proponents pointed to natural gas's role in reducing Pennsylvania's contribution to climate change as cleaner, natural gas-burning power plants displaced coal as the main fuel used for electricity production in the state. However, gas extraction and transportation release methane into the atmosphere that, in the short term, traps even more solar energy than carbon dioxide.[32] Before the shale boom completely reshuffled the state's energy economy, many environmentalists and investors had looked to alternatives to fossil fuels to provide future power. Green Mountain Energy established the state's first wind farm in Somerset County in 2000, and soon giant wind turbines were a common site along the state's ridge lines, especially along the Allegheny Front between State College and the Maryland border (Figure 5.4). The development of wind received a boost from the state in 2004 with the passage of the Alternative Energy Portfolio Standards Act, which required utilities to include an increasing percentage of alternative energy sources. Various incentive programs to encourage the development of wind and solar power over the next fifteen years, however, achieved only limited success as proponents of coal and nuclear power pushed back at perceived threats to their industries and utilities took advantage of regulatory loopholes that allowed them to purchase energy from out-of-state sources rather than investing in new infrastructure. As a result, despite a sevenfold increase in solar power generation and a doubling in wind power between 2010 and 2020, Pennsylvania still ranked a dismal thirty-fifth in the nation for percentage of solar and wind in the state's electricity mix.[33]

As they had for decades, state regulators charged with ensuring public health and abating pollution became lightning rods for both supporters and opponents of natural gas extraction. Despite his background as president of the environmental advocacy group PennFuture, John Hanger, then the secretary of the Department of Environmental Protection (carved from the former Department of Environmental Resources in 1995 along with the DCNR), endorsed the safety of fracking in 2010, declaring, "It's our experience in Pennsylvania that we have not had one case in which the fluids used to break off the gas . . . have returned to contaminate ground water." "There's a lot of focus in the media and the public," he concluded, "on the problems that we have not had." Hanger's strong support for natural gas extraction, if properly regulated, earned him the ire of other environmentalists who wanted to see the practice banned entirely. A decade later, a grand jury report outlined political pressure to allow gas drilling to proceed, including testimony from two former Department of Environmental Protection secretaries, both of whom "felt that the oil and gas industry had its own pipeline to elected officials, and both felt pressure to permit production of shale gas." "It's the government's job to set and enforce the ground rules that protect the public interest," concluded Josh Shapiro, then Pennsylvania's attorney-general, who had commissioned the report. "Through multiple administrations, they failed."[34]

The fight over energy production took place even as the effects of climate change became increasingly apparent and disproportionately affected poor residents and people of color. In 2008, the legislature began requiring the Department of Environmental Protection to study the potential effects of climate change on the economy, ecosystems, and public health. Researchers concluded that rainfall would become more extreme, with "longer dry periods and greater intensity of precipitation when it occurs." Further, the state risked becoming "increasingly unsuitable for many of the tree species" that gave Penn's Woods its name, with the "paper birch, quaking aspen, bigtooth aspen, and yellow birch . . . projected to be extinct [or] greatly reduced, if not eliminated, even under low emissions scenarios." The report also warned of a probable "decline in some of our most valued coldwater communities," including the eastern brook trout, prized as a "recreationally and culturally important species," and an increase of less desirable biological assemblages, "especially invasive species." Finally, the effects of rising average temperatures on agriculture were likely to be varied, with a longer frost-free growing season benefiting the production of some crops even as yields of other commodities, such as apples and potatoes, were likely to decline. Dairy farmers, they suggested, "may experience the greatest challenges from climate change," with reduced crop and forage fields and "animal heat stress" affecting productivity.[35]

Even as the issue of global warming was entangled in growing political polarization, increasing changes to weather in the years that followed the publication of the initial climate impact assessment made the warnings clear to those willing to hear them. Between 2000 and 2020, average annual temperatures rose approximately 1.2 degrees Fahrenheit (0.6 degrees Celsius), and, while the number of very hot days (above 90 degrees Fahrenheit) remained largely the same as the previous century's average, an increase in the frequency of warm nights and decrease in very cold nights demonstrated larger effects in winter and spring compared with summer and fall. These changes fueled the growth of invasive species, often at the expense of charismatic natives, such as eastern hemlocks, Pennsylvania's state tree, which were increasingly attacked by the hemlock woolly adelgid, an Asian species that responds well to a warmer climate.[36]

Beyond agriculture and natural ecosystems, climate change has challenged urban environments and public health. At this point, the most significant climate-related threat to humans remains flooding caused by increased annual precipitation (up about 4.6 inches compared with earlier decades) that often comes in the form of heavy rain, but higher temperatures mean more days with hazardous heat conditions and reduced air quality, increasing the risks of respiratory illness. As with previous examples of environmental inequality, climate change does not affect all Pennsylvanians equally; areas with high concentrations of people of color or those experiencing poverty, for example, are more likely to experience high heat days than the statewide average and less likely to be able to afford air conditioning or other types of mitigation. As the second decade of the twentieth-first century ended, politicians most likely to support regulations limiting greenhouse gas emissions and other climate-change mitigating policies generally represented urban and suburban districts (often Democrats), while rural districts, overwhelmingly represented by Republicans, remained more committed to supporting fossil fuel industries. As a result, it remains unclear whether this generation of Pennsylvanians will be able to muster the type of bipartisan and geographically diverse coalition that will be necessary to tackle the most pressing environmental needs of the age.[37]

———

On Friday, September 30, 2019, the long saga of nuclear power production at Three Mile Island ended. Forty years earlier the site had witnessed the nation's worst commercial nuclear accident, and the plant's closure elicited mixed reactions among residents, which ranged from concerns about the impact of lost jobs and tax revenue to hope that the site would finally be safe once spent fuel was eventually removed. In the end, TMI was unable to compete in a marketplace awash with cheap natural gas—an irony, perhaps, considering the closure of a facility so closely associated with public health and environmental risk resulted in the burning of even more climate change–causing fossil fuels. These are the difficult choices that permeate the working landscapes of twenty-first-century Pennsylvania.[38]

CONCLUSION

The Future of Penn's Woods

I T WAS A BEAUTIFUL AUGUST DAY at Shikellamy State Park when a few dozen current and retired state officials, nonprofit leaders, activists, and lawyers and a couple of academics, including me, gathered to commemorate the fiftieth anniversary of the state's Environmental Rights Amendment. The celebration featured the official opening of Kury Point, an overlook at the confluence of the Susquehanna River's West and North branches that honors Franklin Kury, the state legislator from Sunbury who authored the amendment, along with other key pieces of environmental legislation. Kury, who in 1966 famously won election in a longtime Republican district by denouncing his opponent's opposition to tougher clean water laws, focused his remarks on Pennsylvania's legacy as the cradle of conservation. Pointing westward to the wooded peaks of Bald Eagle State Forest and highlighting the role of Maurice Goddard in advocating for the Project 70 bond issue that expanded Shikellamy State Park itself, Kury concluded: "[When] I ran for the House of Representatives in 1966, I had no idea that anything I might do if elected would be recognized 50 years later. It's a very satisfying moment."[1]

The ceremony's other main speaker, former Pennsylvania Supreme Court Chief Justice Ron Castille, turned his attention to the future of Penn's Woods. In 2013, Castille wrote the plurality opinion overturning key provisions of a state law loosening regulations on natural gas drilling (Act 13) by affirming the Environmental Rights Amendment's guarantee of "clean air, pure water, and to the preservation of the natural, scenic, historic and esthetic values of the environment." After citing the enormous burdens placed on the commonwealth—from the clear-cutting of forests and annihilation of game animals to the Donora Smog, Knox Mine disaster, and Centralia fire— Castille had concluded his opinion by writing: "It is not a historical accident that the Pennsylvania Constitution now places citizens' environmental rights on par with their political rights." Castille noted in his speech that in 2017 a full majority of the state's Supreme Court had reaffirmed his interpretation of the "constitutional public trust" and thus restored "the clear import of the plain language" passed by a four-to-one majority of voters in 1971. As we look forward to the challenges of a warming planet, resurgent fossil fuel use, and need for continued remediation of degraded landscapes, he suggested, Pennsylvania was once again in the vanguard of environmental protection.[2]

As with earlier iterations of conservation in the nineteenth and twentieth centuries, the environmental culture of twenty-first-century Pennsylvania cannot be defined quite as simply as Kury and Castille might suggest. After all, both the 2013 and 2017 rulings were issued by a divided court, and, of course, the legislature passed and the governor signed the regulations allowing fracking to take place and diverted Oil and Gas Fund revenue away from the conservation efforts it was originally intended to support. Further, the enshrinement of environmental rights came from a court increasingly depicted by antienvironmentalists as both partisan and primarily serving the interests of more affluent urban and suburban residents at a greater distance from the largely rural areas that stood to benefit economically from Pennsylvania's resurgence as an energy capital. In this regard, we can draw comparisons with both the struggle by the first generation of professional foresters and game wardens to police traditional activities, such as grazing cattle, hunting deer, and setting fires to increase berry harvests, and Maurice Goddard's campaign to persuade rural residents to support raising funds for Project 70's public land purchases.

Clearly, finding consensus over balancing natural resource consumption and conservation in a state so evenly divided among rural, urban, and suburban communities—not to mention agricultural, manufacturing, and service sectors—remained as difficult as ever. In New York State, where downstream interests enjoyed a virtual lock on state government, Democratic Governor Andrew Cuomo's moratorium on fracking in 2014 was officially codified in the legislature's budget for the 2021 fiscal year. At the same time, Pennsylvania's Democratic Governor Tom Wolf continued to walk a climate change tightrope by committing the state to a Regional Greenhouse Gas Initiative while also supporting the development of Shell's natural gas "cracker" plant in Beaver County, which, he argued, would provide feedstock for "the kind of lightweight products [that a] sustainable energy future is going to require."

Figure C.1 Social distancing with friends on the Rocky Knob Trail, December 2020. (Courtesy: Allen Dieterich-Ward.)

Pennsylvania's Republicans, however, who controlled both houses of the state legislature for all but four of the previous twenty-five years, continued largely to adopt the rhetoric of antienvironmentalism even amid dire warnings about the rapidly warming planet. Finally, the prevalence of anti-mask and anti-vaccine sentiments during the COVID-19 pandemic revealed the extent to which questioning of both public health officials and science itself had taken firm root among many residents in the decades following Rachel Carson's *Silent Spring* and the meltdown at Three Mile Island.[3]

In the end, these strident disagreements over the nature of the state's working landscapes actually make Pennsylvania a pretty good stand-in for the broader environmental debates facing the nation and, indeed, the world. The oversimplification of complex issues into the soundbites that nourish political polarization tends to overshadow broad agreement on a wide range of environmental issues, particularly as you move from the seemingly distant and abstract to the more local and concrete. I was recently talking with a friend, then one of the state's senior conservation administrators, who had just returned from a ribbon cutting at a former railyard site in rural northeastern Pennsylvania that had been transformed into a promenade complete with an ice rink, pedestrian trails, and river access through a "Brownfields to Playfields" initiative. "You wouldn't believe how excited these folks were about their little park," she explained. "At that moment their politics didn't matter. This was an example of how state and local partners could come together to transform an environmental problem into a community asset."[4]

Each day, I think, this basic scenario repeats itself. Virtually no one truly wants to return to the smoky skies, filthy water, and clear-cut landscapes of the past, and efforts to defund conservation programs—from farmland preservation to water and wildlife protection—regularly run into a wall of popular support on state, county, and local levels. The need for social distancing during the COVID-19 pandemic underscored the state's legacy of conservation as millions of residents gained new appreciation for nearby parks, trails, heritage areas, and other public spaces bequeathed to them by previous generations (Figure C.1).[5] It is now apparent that the era of global climate change is no longer in the future but is already upon us in the form of increased flooding, scorching hot summers, and too mild winters and rising numbers of heat-tolerant invasives. Perhaps the Pennsylvanians of the future will look back and find that it was there, in those dark days of fear and loss, that the seeds were planted for a bright new era in the state's environmental history.

NOTES

Introduction

1. *Proceedings of the First Convention of Pennsylvania Foresters, Held at Harrisburg, Pa., March 4, 5, 6, 1908*, bulletin no. 6 (Harrisburg: C. E. Aughinbaugh, 1910); Rachel Jones Williams, "Reviving—and Revising—the Reputation of Ralph Elwood Brock," *Pennsylvania Heritage* 33, no. 4 (Fall 2007), https://paheritage.wpengine.com/article/reviving-revising-reputation-ralph-elwood-brock.

2. Amanda J. DeLorenzo, Ruthann Hubbert-Kemper, and Jason Wilson, *Literature in Stone: The Hundred Year History of Pennsylvania's State Capitol* (Harrisburg: Pennsylvania Capitol Preservation Committee, 2006).

3. J. Donald Hughes, *What Is Environmental History?* (Malden, MA: Polity, 2016). For an extensive listing of Pennsylvania environmental scholarship, see Brian Black and Marcy Ladson, "Pennsylvania Conservation History: An Annotated Bibliography," Pennsylvania Conservation Heritage Project, 2015, https://paconservationheritage.org/resources/bibliographies.

4. For a fuller discussion of these issues within a context similar to Pennsylvania, see David Stradling, *The Nature of New York: An Environmental History of the Empire State* (Ithaca, NY: Cornell University Press, 2010), 2–6.

5. William Conlogue, *Here and There: Reading Pennsylvania's Working Landscapes* (University Park: Penn State University Press, 2013).

6. Constitution of the Commonwealth of Pennsylvania (1968), § 27. Natural Resources and the Public Estate.

Chapter 1

1. Julian Smith, "Meadowcroft Revisited," *American Archaeology Magazine* 26, no. 3 (Fall 2022), https://www.archaeologicalconservancy.org/meadowcroft-revisited.

2. Daniel Richter, *The Ordeal of the Longhouse: The Peoples of the Iroquois League in the Era of European Colonization* (Chapel Hill: University of North Carolina Press, 1992), 9–10. See also Camilla Townsend and Nicky Kay Michael, eds., *On the Turtle's Back: Stories the Lenape Told Their Grandchildren* (New Brunswick, NJ: Rutgers University Press, 2023).

3. Richter, *The Ordeal of the Longhouse*, 10; Daniel Richter, *Native Americans' Pennsylvania* (University Park: Pennsylvania Historical Association, 2005), 10–16.

4. Richter, *The Ordeal of the Longhouse*, 11; Richter, *Native Americans' Pennsylvania*, 16–18; Kenny Copper, "'We Just Want to Be Welcomed Back': The Lenape Seek a Return Home," *WHYY*, accessed July 31, 2023, https://whyy.org/articles/we-just-want-to-be-welcomed-back-the-lenape-seek-a-return-home.

5. Richter, *Native Americans' Pennsylvania*, 19–22; April M. Beisaw, "Environmental History of the Susquehanna Valley around the Time of European Contact," *Pennsylvania History* 79, no. 4 (2012): 368–369.

6. Richter, *Native Americans' Pennsylvania*, 22–26; Beisaw, "Environmental History of the Susquehanna Valley around the Time of European Contact," 369. See also Kurt W. Carr and Roger W. Moeller, *First Pennsylvanians: The Archaeology of Native Americans in Pennsylvania* (Harrisburg: Pennsylvania Historical and Museum Commission, 2015).

7. Richter, *The Ordeal of the Longhouse*, 32–39.

8. Richter, *Native Americans' Pennsylvania*, 26–29; David Stradling, *The Nature of New York: An Environmental History of the Empire State* (Ithaca, NY: Cornell University Press, 2010), 19.

9. Richter, *Native Americans' Pennsylvania*, 38–44; Beisaw, "Environmental History of the Susquehanna Valley around the Time of European Contact," 370–371.

10. Richter, *The Ordeal of the Longhouse*, 11; Richter, *Native Americans' Pennsylvania*, 42–46.

11. Anthony Wallace and Timothy Powell, "How to Buy a Continent: The Protocol of Indian Treaties as Developed by Benjamin Franklin and Other Members of the American Philosophical Society," *Proceedings of the American Philosophical Society* 159, no. 3 (2015): 251–281.

12. William E. Lingelbach, "William Penn and City Planning," *Pennsylvania Magazine of History and Biography* 68, no. 4 (1944): 398–418; Judith A. Ridner, *The Scots Irish of Early Pennsylvania: A Varied People* (Philadelphia: Temple University Press in partnership with the Pennsylvania Historical Association, 2018), 38–57.

13. Christopher R. Dougherty, "Cornwall Archival Survey Project," final report of work performed, Historical Society of Pennsylvania, Philadelphia, March 2009.

14. Sally McMurry, *Pennsylvania Farming: A History in Landscapes* (Pittsburgh: University of Pittsburgh Press, 2017).

15. Ibid., 18; Richard L. Bushman, *The American Farmer in the Eighteenth Century: A Social and Cultural History* (New Haven, CT: Yale University Press, 2018), 140.

16. Bushman, *The American Farmer in the Eighteenth Century*, 149–152; Cumberland County Historical Society, *Water-powered Mills of Cumberland County, Pennsylvania* (Carlisle, PA: Cumberland County Historical Society, 2015); "Historic Context for Transportation Networks in Pennsylvania," report, Pennsylvania State Historic Preservation Office, Harrisburg, 1998, 3–6; Hector St. John de Crèvecoeur, *Letters from an*

American Farmer (London: T. Davies, 1782), https://avalon.law.yale.edu/subject_menus /letters.asp.

17. Gerald G. Eggert, *The Iron Industry in Pennsylvania: With a Listing of National, State, and Private Sites Related to the Pennsylvania Iron Industry and Open to the Public* (Middletown: Pennsylvania Historical Association, 1994), 15.

18. Ibid., 1–5.

19. Ibid., 6–10.

20. Beverly C. Tomek, *Slavery and Abolition in Pennsylvania* (Philadelphia: Temple University Press in partnership with the Pennsylvania Historical Association, 2021), 10; James T. Lemon, *The Best Poor Man's Country: Early Southeastern Pennsylvania* (Baltimore: Johns Hopkins University Press, 2002); John Rutter, "Tracking a Legend," *LancasterOnline*, February 10, 2008, https://lancasteronline.com/news/tracking-a-legend/article _94e83cd9-bf13-5886-9095-ea3974fb0b57.html. On the role of unfree labor in iron furnaces, see also Gerald Eggert, *Making Iron on the Bald Eagle: Roland Curtin's Ironworks and Workers' Community* (University Park: Penn State University Press, 1999).

21. Crèvecoeur, *Letters from an American Farmer*; Therese O'Malley, "Cultivated Lives, Cultivated Spaces: The Scientific Garden in Philadelphia, 1740–1840," and Joel T. Fry, "America's 'Ancient Garden': The Bartram Botanic Garden, 1728–1850," both in *Knowing Nature: Art and Science in Philadelphia, 1740–1840*, ed. Amy R. W. Meyers and Lisa L. Ford (New Haven, CT: Yale University Press, 2011), 60–72.

22. Roger D. Simon, *Philadelphia: A Brief History* (Philadelphia: Temple University Press in partnership with the Pennsylvania Historical Association, 2017), 2–3.

23. Brian Black and Michael J. Chiarappa, eds., *Nature's Entrepôt: Philadelphia's Urban Sphere and Its Environmental Thresholds* (Pittsburgh: University of Pittsburgh Press, 2012), 4–6; David R. Contosta and Carol Franklin, *Metropolitan Paradise: The Struggle for Nature in the City: Philadelphia's Wissahickon Valley, 1620–2020, Volume 1: Wilderness* (Philadelphia: Saint Joseph's University Press, 2010), 94–102.

24. Eric Foner, *Tom Paine and Revolutionary America* (New York: Oxford University Press, 2005), 20; "January 17—Benjamin Franklin, America's First Environmentalist, Born (1706)," *Today in Conservation*, accessed October 6, 2021, https://todayinconserva tion.com/2018/01/january-17-benjamin-franklin-americas-first-environmentalist-born -1706.

25. Gerald J. Kauffman Jr., "The Delaware River Revival: Four Centuries of Historic Water Quality Change from Henry Hudson to Benjamin Franklin to JFK," *Pennsylvania History* 77, no. 4 (Autumn 2010): 432–465; A. Michal McMahon, "'Small Matters': Benjamin Franklin, Philadelphia, and the 'Progress of Cities,'" *Pennsylvania Magazine of History and Biography* 116, no. 2 (1992): 157–182.

26. Meyers and Ford, *Knowing Nature*, 1–4; O'Malley, "Cultivated Lives, Cultivated Spaces"; Fry, "America's 'Ancient Garden.'"

27. Mark Fiege, *The Republic of Nature: An Environmental History of the United States* (Seattle: University of Washington Press, 2012), 70–75; "John Dickinson's 'Farmer' Letters on Their 250th Anniversary," *Independence Institute* (blog), September 22, 2017, https://i2i.org/john-dickinsons-farmer-letters-250th-anniversary.

28. The phrase "shot heard round the world" comes from "Concord Hymn," a poem by Ralph Waldo Emerson written for the 1837 dedication of a monument in Concord, Mas-

sachusetts. Edward Redmond, "Washington as Land Speculator," Library of Congress, Washington, DC, accessed June 29, 2022, https://www.loc.gov/collections/george-wash ington-papers/articles-and-essays/george-washington-survey-and-mapmaker/washing ton-as-land-speculator.

29. "Declaration of Independence: A Transcription," National Archives, November 1, 2015, https://www.archives.gov/founding-docs/declaration-transcript; Matthew C. Ward, *Breaking the Backcountry: The Seven Years' War in Virginia and Pennsylvania, 1754–1765* (Pittsburgh: University of Pittsburgh Press, 2003); Alan Houston, "Wagons for War: How Benjamin Franklin Helped Braddock's March to the Forks," *Western Pennsylvania History* 94, no. 1 (Spring 2011): 23–37.

30. "Declaration of Independence"; Bushman, *The American Farmer in the Eighteenth Century*, 167–182.

31. David Hackett Fischer, *Washington's Crossing* (New York: Oxford University Press, 2004), 94; Blake McGready, "Contested Grounds: An Environmental History of the 1777 Philadelphia Campaign," *Pennsylvania History* 85, no. 1 (2018): 32.

32. Elizabeth A. Fenn, *Pox Americana: The Great Smallpox Epidemic of 1775–82* (New York: Hill and Wang, 2001), 98–99. Ricardo A. Herrera, *Feeding Washington's Army: Surviving the Valley Forge Winter of 1778* (Chapel Hill: University of North Carolina Press, 2022), 50.

33. Colin G. Calloway, *The American Revolution in Indian Country: Crisis and Diversity in Native American Communities* (New York: Cambridge University Press, 1995), 26–54.

34. Ibid., 51. For a discussion of the applicability of the concept of settler colonialism to the environmental history of early Pennsylvania, see Michael Dean Mackintosh, "The Contested Ground of the 'Peaceable Kingdom': Environmental Change and the Construction of Identity in Early Pennsylvania" (Ph.D. diss., Temple University, Philadelphia, 2022), 28–31.

Chapter 2

1. Charles Dickens, *American Notes for General Circulation* (London: Chapman and Hall, Ltd., 1913), 121–130.

2. Ibid., 128–129; William Shank, *Indian Trails to Superhighways* (York, PA: American Canal and Transportation Center, 1974).

3. Christopher F. Jones, *Routes of Power: Energy and Modern America* (Cambridge, MA: Harvard University Press, 2014), 29–30.

4. Robert J. Kapsch, *Over the Alleghenies: Early Canals and Railroads of Pennsylvania* (Morgantown: West Virginia University Press, 2013).

5. Albert J. Churella, *The Pennsylvania Railroad*, vol. 1 (Philadelphia: University of Pennsylvania Press, 2013), 38–39.

6. Cumberland County Historical Society, *Water-powered Mills of Cumberland County, Pennsylvania* (Carlisle, PA: The Society, 2015); Kapsch, *Over the Alleghenies*.

7. U.S. National Park Service, "Hollidaysburg Canal Basin," Allegheny Portage Railroad National Historic Site, accessed September 28, 2021, https://www.nps.gov/alpo/learn /historyculture/hburgbasin.htm.

8. Philip Holbrook Nicklin, *A Pleasant Peregrination through the Prettiest Parts of*

Pennsylvania (Philadelphia: Grigg and Elliott, 1836), 62; U.S. National Park Service, "Hollidaysburg Canal Basin."

9. John C. Paige, *Pennsylvania Railroad Shops and Works, Altoona, Pennsylvania* (Denver: America's Industrial Heritage Project, National Park Service, 1989); Churella, *The Pennsylvania Railroad*, 10.

10. Sally McMurry, *Pennsylvania Farming: A History in Landscapes* (Pittsburgh: University of Pittsburgh Press, 2017), 40.

11. William Milnor Roberts, *Report of William Milnor Roberts, Chief Engineer of the Cumberland Valley Rail Road Company: Made to the Board, on 23rd Oct. 1835* (Annapolis: Jeremiah Hughes, 1836), 4; McMurry, *Pennsylvania Farming*, 103–104.

12. Frances Milton Trollope, *Domestic Manners of the Americans* (London: Whittaker, Treacher, 1832), chap. 26, https://www.gutenberg.org/cache/epub/10345/pg10345.html; Dickens, *American Notes for General Circulation*, chap. 7.

13. Roger D. Simon, *Philadelphia: A Brief History* (Philadelphia: Temple University Press in partnership with the Pennsylvania Historical Association, 2017), 25.

14. Edward Muller and Joel Tarr, "The Interaction of Natural and Built Landscapes in the Pittsburgh Landscape," in *Devastation and Renewal: An Environmental History of Pittsburgh and Its Region*, ed. Joel Tarr (Pittsburgh: University of Pittsburgh Press, 2003), 15–16.

15. Emma Lapsansky-Werner, "Building Democratic Communities, 1800–1850," in *Pennsylvania: A History of the Commonwealth*, ed. Randall Miller and William Pencak (University Park: Pennsylvania State University Press, 2002), 158–171; David G. McCullough, *The Johnstown Flood* (New York: Simon and Schuster, 2004).

16. Char Miller, *Gifford Pinchot and the Making of Modern Environmentalism* (Washington, DC: Island Press/Shearwater Books, 2001), 20–27.

17. Gerald Eggert, *Harrisburg Industrializes: The Coming of Factories to an American Community* (University Park: Pennsylvania State University Press, 1993).

18. Jones, *Routes of Power*, 23–58.

19. "Lehigh Canal Historical Marker," ExplorePAHistory.com, October 21, 1995, https://explorepahistory.com/hmarker.php?markerId=1-A-B6; C. Gregory Knight, Paul E. Shaw, and Judith Kiusalaas, "Pennsylvania Anthracite," in *Pennsylvania Coal: Resources, Technology, and Utilization*, ed. Shyamal K. Majumdar and E. Willard Miller (Easton: Pennsylvania Academy of Science, 1983), 43–50. The history of iron, steel, and energy production in Pennsylvania is strongly connected with an expanding literature on the history of capitalism: see, e.g., Thomas Foley, "'An Odious Aristocracy': Energy, Politics, and the Roots of Industrial Capitalism in Nineteenth Century Pennsylvania" (Ph.D. diss., Georgetown University, Washington, DC, 2019); Paul Sabin, "'A Dive into Nature's Great Grab-bag': Nature, Gender and Capitalism in the Early Pennsylvania Oil Industry," *Pennsylvania History* 66, no. 4 (1999): 472–505.

20. Simon, *Philadelphia*; Edward K. Muller and Joel A. Tarr, eds., *Making Industrial Pittsburgh Modern: Environment, Landscape, Transportation, Energy and Planning* (Pittsburgh: University of Pittsburgh Press, 2019), 123.

21. Ann Norton Greene, *Horses at Work: Harnessing Power in Industrial America* (Cambridge, MA: Harvard University Press, 2008), 172–173; Clay McShane and Joel A. Tarr, *The Horse in the City: Living Machines in the Nineteenth Century* (Baltimore: Johns Hopkins University Press, 2007).

22. James E. Higgins, *The Health of the Commonwealth: A Brief History of Medicine, Public Health, and Disease in Pennsylvania* (Philadelphia: Temple University Press in partnership with the Pennsylvania Historical Association, 2020); Simon, *Philadelphia*, 41–42.

23. Joel A. Tarr and Terry F. Yosie, "Critical Decisions in Pittsburgh Water and Wastewater Treatment," in Tarr, *Devastation and Renewal*; Higgins, *The Health of the Commonwealth*, 26–29; G. F. Pyle, "The Diffusion of Cholera in the United States in the Nineteenth Century," *Geographical Analysis* 1, no. 1 (1969): 59–75; Morris A. Pierce, "Allentown, Pennsylvania Waterworks," *Documentary History of American Water-works*, 2015, accessed July 9, 2023, http://www.waterworkshistory.us/PA/Allentown.

24. Muriel Earley Sheppard, *Cloud by Day: The Story of Coal and Coke and People*, repr. ed. (Pittsburgh: University of Pittsburgh Press, 1991), 1.

25. Eric Rutkow, *American Canopy: Trees, Forests, and the Making of a Nation* (New York: Scribner, 2014); Ronald Elroy Ostman and Harry Littell, *Wood Hicks and Bark Peelers: A Visual History of Pennsylvania's Railroad Lumbering Communities: The Photographic Legacy of William T. Clarke* (University Park: Pennsylvania State University Press, 2016), 22–25.

26. Ostman and Littell, *Wood Hicks and Bark Peelers*, 36–42; PA Heritage Staff, "Barnhart Log Loader at Pennsylvania Lumber Museum," *Pennsylvania Heritage* 23, no. 3 (Summer 2003), https://paheritage.wpengine.com/article/barnhart-log-loader-pennsylvania-lumber-museum.

27. Ostman and Littell, *Wood Hicks and Bark Peelers*, 28–29, 42–52; Michael A. Leeson and Maybel Hull Swanson, *History of the Counties of McKean, Elk, Cameron and Potter, Pennsylvania with Biographical Selections* (Chicago: J. H. Beers, 1890), 1127–1130.

28. Churella, *The Pennsylvania Railroad*, 284–293.

29. Allen Dieterich-Ward, *Beyond Rust: Metropolitan Pittsburgh and the Fate of Industrial America* (Philadelphia: University of Pennsylvania Press, 2016), 35–37.

30. Ibid., 48.

31. Brian Black, *Petrolia: The Landscape of America's First Oil Boom* (Baltimore: Johns Hopkins University Press, 2000), 25–26; Jones, *Routes of Power*, 89–121, quote on 116.

32. Black, *Petrolia*, 60–81, 138; Carola Hein, "Refineries (Oil)," *The Encyclopedia of Greater Philadelphia*, accessed August 13, 2022, https://philadelphiaencyclopedia.org/essays/refineries-oil.

33. Jones, *Routes of Power*, 12.

Chapter 3

1. Mary S. Lundy, "Sketch of the Forestry Movement in Philadelphia," *Forest Leaves*, July 1886, 1.

2. Susan Rimby, *Mira Lloyd Dock and the Progressive Era Conservation Movement* (University Park: Pennsylvania State University Press, 2012), 42.

3. Roger Simon, *Philadelphia: A Brief History* (Philadelphia: Temple University Press in partnership with the Pennsylvania Historical Association, 2017), 52–54.

4. "Pennsylvania Politics, 1865–1930: Pennsylvania's Bosses and Political Machines," *Stories from PA History*, accessed July 9, 2023, https://explorepahistory.com/story.php?storyId=1-9-20&chapter=1; John Bauman and Edward Muller, *Before Renaissance: Planning in Pittsburgh, 1889–1943* (Pittsburgh: University of Pittsburgh Press, 2006), 23.

5. Simon, *Philadelphia*, 67–68; Ernest Morrison, *J. Horace McFarland: A Thorn for Beauty* (Harrisburg: Pennsylvania Historical and Museum Commission, 1995), 79; Thomas Wirth, "Urban Neglect: The Environment, Public Health, and Influenza in Philadelphia, 1915–1919," *Pennsylvania History* 73, no. 3 (2006): 317.

6. Rimby, *Mira Lloyd Dock and the Progressive Era Conservation Movement*, 97. The classic overview of Progressive urban environmental reform is William H. Wilson, *The City Beautiful Movement* (Baltimore: Johns Hopkins University Press, 1994).

7. Rimby, *Mira Lloyd Dock and the Progressive Era Conservation Movement*, 43; Morrison, *J. Horace McFarland*, 73.

8. Gertrude Biddle, "The Story of the Civic Club of Carlisle," *Chautauquan* 37 (August 1903): 503–505; Rimby, *Mira Lloyd Dock and the Progressive Era Conservation Movement*, 98.

9. Simon, *Philadelphia*, 68–69.

10. Morrison, *J. Horace McFarland*, 80–82.

11. Ibid., 82–83, 96.

12. Bauman and Muller, *Before Renaissance*, 30; Simon, *Philadelphia*, 68; Rachel Williams, "History and Memory of the Old Eighth Ward," *Pennsylvania History* 87, no. 1 (Winter 2020): 166.

13. Rimby, *Mira Lloyd Dock and the Progressive Era Conservation Movement*, 52–54.

14. Peter Linehan, "Saving Penn's Woods: Deforestation and Reforestation in Pennsylvania," *Pennsylvania Legacies* 10, no. 1 (May 2010): 20–25; Sally McMurry, *Pennsylvania Farming: A History in Landscapes* (Pittsburgh: University of Pittsburgh Press, 2017), 185.

15. David Stradling, *The Nature of New York: An Environmental History of the Empire State* (Ithaca, NY: Cornell University Press, 2010), 100–105.

16. Char Miller, *Gifford Pinchot and the Making of Modern Environmentalism* (Washington, DC: Island Press/Shearwater Books, 2001), 19, 338.

17. *From the Schuylkill to the Hudson: Landscapes of the Early American Republic* (Philadelphia: Pennsylvania Academy of the Fine Arts, 2019), 15; Stradling, *The Nature of New York*, 77–79, 146.

18. John P. Lundy, *The Saranac Exiles: A Winter's Tale of the Adirondacks* (Philadelphia: [J. P. Lundy], 1880), 39, http://archive.org/details/saranacexileswin00lund; John P. Lundy, "Forests Not Exclusively for Human Use," *Forest Leaves*, December 1890, 51–53.

19. Charles A. Hardy III, "Fish or Foul: A History of the Delaware River Basin through the Perspective of the American Shad, 1682 to the Present," *Pennsylvania History* 66, no. 4 (1999): 506–534; Joe Kosack, *The Pennsylvania Game Commission, 1895–1995: 100 Years of Wildlife Conservation* (Harrisburg: Pennsylvania Game Commission, 1995), 15–26.

20. Pennsylvania General Assembly, "Appropriating Grounds for Public Purposes," Public Law 547, no. 525 (1867); Elizabeth Milroy, "'Pro Bono Publico': Ecology, History, and the Creation of Philadelphia's Fairmount Park System," in *Nature's Entrepôt: Philadelphia's Urban Sphere and Its Environmental Thresholds*, ed. Brian Black and Michael Chiarappa (Pittsburgh: University of Pittsburgh Press, 2012); Lundy, *The Saranac Exiles*, 50.

21. Rebecca Swanger, "'Something akin to a Second Birth': Joseph Trimble Rothrock and the Formation of the Forestry Movement in Pennsylvania, 1839–1922," *Pennsylvania Magazine of History and Biography* 134, no. 4 (October 2010): 339–363.

22. Lester A. DeCoster, *The Legacy of Penn's Woods: A History of the Pennsylvania Bureau of Forestry* (Harrisburg: Pennsylvania Historical and Museum Commission, 1995), 27–30;

Ellen A. Manno, Kim C. Steiner, and R. Alexander Day, "Ralph E. Brock and the State Forest Academy at Mont Alto, Pennsylvania," *Forest History Today* (Fall 2002): 12–19.

23. Kosack, *The Pennsylvania Game Commission*, 15–30; Kenneth Wolensky, *To Protect, Conserve, and Enhance: The History of the Pennsylvania Fish and Boat Commission* (Harrisburg: Pennsylvania Fish and Boat Commission, 2016), 59.

24. Kosack, *The Pennsylvania Game Commission*, 38.

25. Martha Moon-Renton, "Michaux State Forest: Conservation vs. Crime," unpublished paper, Shippensburg University, Shippensburg, PA, 2023; DeCoster, *The Legacy of Penn's Woods*, 34–35; Charles D. Bonsted, oral history interview with George H. Wirt, March 1959, https://foresthistory.org/wp-content/uploads/2016/12/Wirt.pdf. These types of issues are covered in Karl Jacoby, *Crimes against Nature: Squatters, Poachers, Thieves, and the Hidden History of American Conservation* (Berkeley: University of California Press, 2014).

26. Valencia Libby, "Jane Haines' Vision: The Pennsylvania School of Horticulture for Women," *Journal of the New England Garden History Society* 10 (2002): 44–52.

27. DeCoster, *The Legacy of Penn's Woods*, 42–46.

28. Ibid., 67–69; "Motor Routes to Allegheny Forest," *Philadelphia Inquirer*, August 30, 1925, 19.

29. DeCoster, *The Legacy of Penn's Woods*, 45–48; Rachel Jones Williams, "Reviving—and Revising—the Reputation of Ralph Elwood Brock," *Pennsylvania Heritage* 33, no. 4 (Fall 2007), https://paheritage.wpengine.com/article/reviving-revising-reputation-ralph-elwood-brock. On the history of the American chestnut, see Donald Davis, *The American Chestnut: An Environmental History* (Athens: University of Georgia Press, 2021).

30. Cheyney M. Thomas, "Camp Milroy," *Philadelphia Tribune*, February 15, March 1, March 29, April 12, 1934; William Bryant, "Camp Milroy," *Philadelphia Tribune*, May 17, 1934.

31. McMurry, *Pennsylvania Farming*, 185–186.

32. Joseph M. Speakman, *At Work in Penn's Woods: The Civilian Conservation Corps in Pennsylvania* (University Park: Pennsylvania State University Press, 2006), 14–18.

33. Ibid., 30–35; "Veterans of C.C.C. Reunite in Forest," *New York Times*, September 11, 1983, 64.

34. Speakman, *At Work in Penn's Woods*, 90–95; Bryant, "Camp Milroy"; Thomas, "Camp Milroy" (March 1, April 12, 1934); "Veterans of C.C.C. Reunite in Forest," 64.

35. Speakman, *At Work in Penn's Woods*, 95–100; "C.C.C. Milroy, Pa.," *Philadelphia Tribune*, January 24, 1935; "News from C.C.C. at Milroy," *Philadelphia Tribune*, August 8, 1935; "C.C.C. Camp Milroy, Pa.: 'Ramblings,'" *Philadelphia Tribune*, October 10, 1935.

36. Speakman, *At Work in Penn's Woods*, 99–100; Simon, *Philadelphia*, 76–77; "Projects in Pennsylvania," *Living New Deal*, accessed November 19, 2021, https://livingnewdeal.org/us/pa.

37. "Projects in Pennsylvania"; Bauman and Muller, *Before Renaissance*, 194–226.

38. "Projects in Pennsylvania."

39. George Swetnam, *Pennsylvania Transportation* (Gettysburg: Pennsylvania Historical Association, 1968), 69–70.

40. Ibid., 72–75.

Chapter 4

1. Mark H. Lytle, *The Gentle Subversive: Rachel Carson, Silent Spring, and the Rise of the Environmental Movement* (New York: Oxford University Press, 2007), 2; Rachel Carson, *Silent Spring*, 40th anniversary ed. (Boston: Houghton Mifflin, 2002), 1–3.

2. Lizabeth Cohen, *A Consumer's Republic: The Politics of Mass Consumption in Postwar America* (New York: Alfred A. Knopf, 2003), 8–9, 83; "The Silent Spring of Rachel Carson," broadcast, *CBS Reports*, April 3, 1963. The concluding quote is from the Constitution of the Commonwealth of Pennsylvania (1968), sec. 27, Natural Resources and the Public Estate.

3. Christopher Sellers, "Suburban Nature, Class, and Environmentalism in Levittown," in *Second Suburb: Levittown, Pennsylvania*, ed. Dianne Harris (Pittsburgh: University of Pittsburgh Press, 2010).

4. Charles Hardy, "The Watering of Philadelphia," *Pennsylvania Heritage*, Spring 2004, http://paheritage.wpengine.com/article/watering-philadelphia; Andrew T. McPhee, *The Donora Death Fog: Clean Air and the Tragedy of a Pennsylvania Mill Town* (Pittsburgh: University of Pittsburgh Press, 2023).

5. Allen Dieterich-Ward, *Beyond Rust: Metropolitan Pittsburgh and the Fate of Industrial America* (Philadelphia: University of Pennsylvania Press, 2016), 3–4; Angela Gugliotta, "How, When and for Whom Was Smoke a Problem in Pittsburgh?" in *Devastation and Renewal: An Environmental History of Pittsburgh and Its Region*, ed. Joel Tarr (Pittsburgh: University of Pittsburgh Press, 2003).

6. Roger Simon, *Philadelphia: A Brief History* (Philadelphia: Temple University Press in partnership with the Pennsylvania Historical Association, 2017), 81–87.

7. David Schuyler, *A City Transformed: Redevelopment, Race, and Suburbanization in Lancaster, Pennsylvania, 1940–1980* (University Park: Pennsylvania State University Press, 2002).

8. Jeff Wiltse, *Contested Waters: A Social History of Swimming Pools in America* (Chapel Hill: University of North Carolina Press, 2007). The quote is from Jeff Wiltse, "Swimming against Segregation: The Struggle to Desegregate," *Pennsylvania Legacies* 10, no. 2 (November 2010): 12–17.

9. Sally McMurry, *Pennsylvania Farming: A History in Landscapes* (Pittsburgh: University of Pittsburgh Press, 2017), 337–345; Shyamal K. Majumdar and E. Willard Miller, eds., *Pennsylvania Coal: Resources, Technology, and Utilization* (Easton: Pennsylvania Academy of Science, 1983), 351–354, 472–475.

10. Thomas G. Smith, *Green Republican: John Saylor and the Preservation of America's Wilderness* (Pittsburgh: University of Pittsburgh Press, 2006), 44, 158–179. See also J. Brooks Flippen, *Conservative Conservationist: Russell E. Train and the Emergence of American Environmentalism* (Baton Rouge: Louisiana State University Press, 2006).

11. William C. Forrey, *History of Pennsylvania's State Parks*, vol. 1 (Harrisburg: Pennsylvania Bureau of State Parks, 1984), 36.

12. Lester DeCoster, *The Legacy of Penn's Woods: A History of the Pennsylvania Bureau of Forestry* (Harrisburg: Pennsylvania Historical and Museum Commission, 1995), 84.

13. Forrey, *History of Pennsylvania's State Parks*, 41–53.

14. Lindsay Phillips, Ed Charles, and R. J. Phiambolis, "PA Environment Timeline," 2015, http://paconservationheritage.org/wp-content/uploads/A-Timeline-of-Environmen

tal-History.pdf; Kasia Kopec, "Pumping Leads to Disaster," *Times Leader* (Wilkes-Barre), December 7, 2003.

15. Another disaster related to coal mining that drew public attention was the Centralia fire, which began burning in 1962 and eventually forced the entire community's evacuation. See Joan Quigley, *The Day the Earth Caved In: An American Mining Tragedy* (New York: Random House, 2009); David DeKok, *Fire Underground: The Ongoing Tragedy of the Centralia Mine Fire* (Guilford, CT: Globe Pequot Press, 2010).

16. Phillips et al., "PA Environment Timeline"; Kopec, "Pumping Leads to Disaster."

17. Franklin Kury, *Clean Politics, Clean Streams: A Legislative Autobiography and Reflections* (Bethlehem, PA: Lehigh University Press, 2011), 72.

18. Ibid., 27–40.

19. Tony M. Guerrieri, Sakura Ung, and Coleen P. Engvall, "Legislative and Oversight Accomplishments of Pennsylvania's Joint Legislative Air and Water Pollution Control and Conservation Committee: A 50-Year Retrospective," December 2018, http://paconserva tionheritage.org/wp-content/uploads/joint-committee-50-year-retrospective.pdf.

20. Kury, *Clean Politics, Clean Streams*, 59–68.

21. "Biography: Ruth Patrick," Drexel University, accessed December 29, 2022, http:// ansp.org/research/environmental-research/people/patrick/biography. "Report of the Committee of Conference on House Bill 926," Printer's No. 3422, Pennsylvania House of Representatives, 1967–1968 sess.

22. Adam Rome, *The Genius of Earth Day: How a 1970 Teach-In Unexpectedly Made the First Green Generation* (New York: Hill and Wang, 2013); "Philadelphia Earth Week, Fifty Years On," Science History Institute, April 21, 2020, https://www.sciencehistory .org/distillations/philadelphia-earth-week-fifty-years-on; Dann Noonan, "Pollution More than Just Linear Problem," "Today's Activities," and "Join the Environmental Fight," all in *The Slate*, Shippensburg State College, Shippensburg, PA, April 22, 1970.

23. James Longhurst, *Citizen Environmentalists* (Medford, MA: Tufts University Press, 2010), 3–4; Alexandra Straub, "Environmental Movement," *The Encyclopedia of Greater Philadelphia*, accessed December 17, 2021, https://philadelphiaencyclopedia.org/essays /environmental-movement; "PEC at 50: 'We Had to Do Something,'" Pennsylvania Environmental Council, accessed August 13, 2021, https://pecpa.org/pec-blog/pec-at-50-we -had-to-do-something.

24. Guerrieri et al., "Legislative and Oversight Accomplishments of Pennsylvania's Joint Legislative Air and Water Pollution Control and Conservation Committee," 12.

25. Kury, *Clean Politics, Clean Streams*, 69–72.

26. Ibid., 121–122; Bill O'Boyle, "Agnes Now a Flood of Memories," *Times Leader* (Wilkes-Barre), February 15, 2013. See also Timothy W. Kneeland, *Playing Politics with Natural Disaster: Hurricane Agnes, the 1972 Election, and the Origins of FEMA* (Ithaca, NY: Cornell University Press, 2020).

27. DeCoster, *The Legacy of Penn's Woods*, 86–89.

28. Kenneth Wolensky, *To Protect, Conserve, and Enhance: The History of the Pennsylvania Fish and Boat Commission* (Harrisburg: Pennsylvania Fish and Boat Commission, 2016).

29. Dyana Z. Furmansky, *Rosalie Edge, Hawk of Mercy: The Activist Who Saved Nature from the Conservationists* (Athens: University of Georgia Press, 2010); Joe Kosack, *The Pennsylvania Game Commission, 1895–1995: 100 Years of Wildlife Conservation* (Harris-

burg: Pennsylvania Game Commission, 1995), 136–141. The commission reintroduced limited hunting for bobcats in 2000.

30. Kury, *Clean Politics, Clean Streams*, 121–142.

31. Meg Jacobs, *Panic at the Pump: The Energy Crisis and the Transformation of American Politics in the 1970s* (New York: Hill and Wang, 2016).

32. David A. Milne, "Clean Streams Are on the Increase," *News Herald* (Franklin), April 30, 1973.

33. Ernest Morrison, *A Walk on the Downhill Side of the Log: The Life of Maurice K. Goddard* (Mechanicsburg: Pennsylvania Forestry Association, 2000), 224–228; Allen Dieterich-Ward, "'We've Got Jobs. Let's Fight for Them': Coal, Clean Air, and the Politics of Antienvironmentalism," *Ohio Valley History* 17, no. 1 (Spring 2017): 6–28.

34. William M. Eichbaum, "The Environmental Pollution Strike Force: A Brief History," Summer 2018, unpublished paper, 7–9; Longhurst, *Citizen Environmentalists*, 163.

35. "Roadway Is Classic Subject of Controversy," *Morning Herald/Evening Standard* (Uniontown), Mar. 24, 1975; "Pa. House, DER Battle Escalates," *Lebanon Daily News*, June 24, 1976; "Legislature, DER to Meet Again," *Daily Intelligencer* (Doylestown), July 23, 1976; David A. Milne, "Principle Move: DER Watchdog Offers Career to Save Legal Strike Force," *Daily Intelligencer* (Doylestown), July 13, 1976.

36. "Dr. Goddard Confirmed as Secretary of Environmental Resources," *Warren Time-Mirror and Observer*, November 9, 1971; Morrison, *A Walk on the Downhill Side of the Log*, 237; Joy Ann Bilharz, *The Allegany Senecas and Kinzua Dam: Forced Relocation through Two Generations* (Lincoln: University of Nebraska Press, 1998); Maurice K. Goddard, "Kinzua Dam Upheld: Suggested Alternative is Declared Economically Impractical," letter to the editor, *New York Times*, March 26, 1960; Allan Forbes, dir., *Lands of Our Ancestors*, documentary, Seneca Nation of New York, 2013.

37. Scoop Lewis, "Tocks Controversy Still Hot," *Bucks County Courier Times*, April 5, 1975.

38. Kury, *Clean Politics, Clean Streams*, 121–142.

Chapter 5

1. Dick Thornburgh, "Three Mile Island," speech delivered to the National Press Club, Washington, DC, March 28, 1989. See also J. Samuel Walker, *Three Mile Island: A Nuclear Crisis in Historical Perspective* (Berkeley: University of California Press, 2005); Natasha Zaretsky, *Radiation Nation: Three Mile Island and the Political Transformation of the 1970s* (New York: Columbia University Press, 2018).

2. Ronald Reagan, "Inaugural Address," Washington, DC, January 20, 1981.

3. Robert Rowthorn and Ramana Ramaswamy, "Deindustrialization—Its Causes and Implications," *Economic Issues*, International Monetary Fund, September 1997; James G. Gimpel, *Separate Destinations: Migration, Immigration, and the Politics of Places* (Ann Arbor: University of Michigan Press, 1999), 238–279; Peter Perl, "Union Leaders Tour Rusted 'Mon Valley,'" *Washington Post*, August 13, 1985.

4. Allen Dieterich-Ward, "'We've Got Jobs. Let's Fight for Them': Coal, Clean Air, and the Politics of Antienvironmentalism," *Ohio Valley History* 17, no. 1 (Spring 2017): 6–28; Dick Thornburgh, *Where the Evidence Leads: An Autobiography* (Pittsburgh: University of Pittsburgh Press, 2003), 128–129, 163–165. See also James Morton Turner and

Andrew C. Isenberg, *The Republican Reversal: Conservatives and the Environment from Nixon to Trump* (Cambridge: Harvard University Press, 2018).

5. "Impact of State Parks on Pennsylvania's Economy," Pennsylvania Department of Environmental Resources, Harrisburg, 1990; Tom Gilbert, "Pennsylvania's Return on Investment in the Keystone Recreation, Park, and Conservation Fund," Trust for Public Land, Philadelphia, 2013.

6. The agency was renamed the Pennsylvania Fish and Boat Commission in 1991.

7. Charles A. Hardy III, "Fish or Foul: A History of the Delaware River Basin through the Perspective of the American Shad, 1682 to the Present," *Pennsylvania History* 66, no. 4 (1999): 506–534; Joe Kosack, *The Pennsylvania Game Commission, 1895–1995: 100 Years of Wildlife Conservation* (Harrisburg: Pennsylvania Game Commission, 1995), 136.

8. Thomas Daniels, "An Analysis of the Economic Impact of Pennsylvania's Farmland Preservation Program," Pennsylvania Department of Agriculture, Harrisburg, September 27, 2019. Pennsylvania also had an important role in another response to the changes in postwar agricultural landscapes, organic farming: see Andrew Case and Paul Sutter, *The Organic Profit: Rodale and the Making of Marketplace Environmentalism* (Seattle: University of Washington Press, 2018).

9. Governor's Press Office, "U.S. EPA Administrator William Ruckelshaus and Others Commemorate Signing of Regional Agreement to Cleanup Chesapeake Bay," press release, December 13, 1984, https://digital.library.pitt.edu/islandora/object/pitt%3Aais9830 .11.02.1495/viewer; "Waters at Risk: Pollution in the Susquehanna Watershed—Sources and Solutions," report, Chesapeake Bay Foundation, Harrisburg, June 2006; Tom Horton, "Chesapeake Is a Victim of Pennsylvania Fiasco," *The Sun* (Baltimore), December 5, 1992. Pollution numbers are from 2006.

10. Horton, "Chesapeake Is a Victim of Pennsylvania Fiasco"; "House Bill 496 Receives Strong Opposition," *Wayne Independent*, May 19, 1992; Philip Favero and Charles Adballa, "Creating Workable Implementation Rules to Meet the Complexities of Manure Management: Pennsylvania's Nutrient Management Law," *Journal of Soil and Water Conservation* 52, no. 5 (September 1, 1997): 320–323.

11. "Thornburgh Considering Incentives to Promote Coal Usage," *Kittanning Leader-Times*, January 24, 1980; Shyamal K. Majumdar and E. Willard Miller, eds., *Pennsylvania Coal: Resources, Technology, and Utilization* (Easton: Pennsylvania Academy of Science, 1983), iv; Kris Maher, "Town Hopes to Keep Tower of Coal Power," *Wall Street Journal*, March 12, 2012.

12. Governor's Press Office, "Letter to EPA re. Acid Rain," October 16, 1984, https:// digital.library.pitt.edu/islandora/object/pitt:ais9830.11.02.1453; "Fish Endangered, Study Claims Acid Rain Killed Laurel Hill Trout," *Indiana Gazette*, April 6, 1984.

13. "Acid Rain in State Growing Worse, Groups Say," *Dubois Courier Express*, November 7, 1986; Dick Thornburgh, "Our Blue Planet: A Law Enforcement Challenge," keynote address delivered at the Department of Justice Environmental Law Conference, New Orleans, January 8, 1991.

14. Thomas Murphy, "Guest Editorial," *Executive Report*, January 1990; Don Hopey, "World Meeting on Rail-to-Trails Set Here," *Pittsburgh Post-Gazette*, January 31, 1998; Don Hopey, "Signs of Changing Times-Riverfront Trail Markers Point the Way to Greener Future," *Pittsburgh Post-Gazette*, June 22, 1999.

15. Stephen Nepa, "Superfund Sites," *The Encyclopedia of Greater Philadelphia*, ac-

cessed December 17, 2021, https://philadelphiaencyclopedia.org/archive/superfund-sites; Ramona Smith and Joe O'Dowd, "Publicker Fire Closes Bridge," *Philadelphia Daily News*, April 11, 1992.

16. Joel Tarr, "Pittsburgh and the Manufactured Gas Industry," *Pittsburgh Engineer*, Winter 2006, 12–15; Charles Bartsch, "Analysis of Pennsylvania's Brownfields Program," Northeast-Midwest Institute, Washington, DC, December 2003

17. "Brownfield Development Guide," Pennsylvania Department of Environmental Protection, Harrisburg, November 2021; "Brownfield Redevelopment; Success Stories," Pennsylvania Department of Environmental Protection, Harrisburg, accessed August 31, 2021, https://www.dep.pa.gov:443/Business/Land/Redevelopment/Pages/Success-Stories .aspx; Eric Deabill and Jayne Ann Bugda, "Borough Officials Consider Zoning Change for Taylor Colliery," WBRE/WYOU-TV, August 8, 2018, https://www.pahomepage.com /news/borough-officials-consider-zoning-change-for-taylor-colliery.

18. Allen Dieterich-Ward, *Beyond Rust: Metropolitan Pittsburgh and the Fate of Industrial America* (Philadelphia: University of Pennsylvania Press, 2016), 183, 212; Michaelle Bond, "Philadelphia Is a Leader in Turning Old Factories and Offices into Apartments," *Philadelphia Inquirer*, November 4, 2021.

19. "Assembly OKs Pine Creek Bill," *Trailblazing in Pennsylvania* (Rails-to-Trails Conservancy), no. 2, Summer 1990; Laura Bly, "Ten Great Places to Take a Bike Tour," *USA Today*, July 27, 2001; Carl Knoch and Patricia Tomes, "Pine Creek Rail Trail 2006 User Survey and Economic Impact Analysis" (Washington, DC: Rails-to-Trails Conservancy, December 2006).

20. Edward K. Muller, ed., *An Uncommon Passage: Traveling through History on the Great Allegheny Passage Trail* (Pittsburgh: University of Pittsburgh Press, 2009), 245–266.

21. Arthur Ziegler, "Preservation as a Tool for Achieving Economic Vitality," *Pittsburgh History and Landmarks Foundation* (blog), August 31, 2012, https://phlf.org/2012/08/31 /arthur-ziegler-preservation-as-a-tool-for-achieving-economic-vitality; Diane Sicotte, *From Workshop to Waste Magnet: Environmental Inequality in the Philadelphia Region* (New Brunswick: Rutgers University Press, 2016).

22. Sicotte, *From Workshop to Waste Magnet*, 131–135.

23. U.S. Environmental Protection Agency Region III and Pennsylvania Department of Environmental Resources, "Environmental Risk Study for City of Chester, Pennsylvania (Summary Report)," Philadelphia, June 1995; Rick Kearns, "Chester Lawsuit Declared Moot by U.S. Supreme Court," October 6, 1998, http://www.ejnet.org/chester/moot.html.

24. Tim Lambert, "For Shanksville Landowner, Downing of Flight 93 on Sept. 11 is Personal," National Public Radio, September 9, 2016, https://www.npr.org/2016/09/09 /493228738/for-shanksville-landowner-downing-of-flight-93-on-sept-11-is-personal.

25. Valley Forge was transferred to the NPS during the American Bicentennial in 1976.

26. Eleanor Mahoney, "History of the Pennsylvania Heritage Areas," Pennsylvania Department of Conservation and Natural Resources, Harrisburg, 2014, 15–23.

27. Ernest Morrison, *A Walk on the Downhill Side of the Log: The Life of Maurice K. Goddard* (Mechanicsburg: The Pennsylvania Forestry Association, 2000), 294–296; Mahoney, "History of the Pennsylvania Heritage Areas," 26; Carolyn Kitch, *Pennsylvania in Public Memory: Reclaiming the Industrial Past* (University Park: Pennsylvania State University Press, 2012), 41.

28. Kitch, *Pennsylvania in Public Memory*, 43; "Pennsylvania Conservation Landscapes: Models of Successful Collaboration," Pennsylvania Department of Conservation and Natural Resources, Harrisburg, 2019, 4. The other six CLIs are Kittatinny Ridge, Laurel Highlands, Lehigh Valley Greenways, Pocono Forests and Waters, Schuylkill Highlands, and South Mountain.

29. "Range Resources Celebrates 25 Years in Pennsylvania," Range Resources, March 9, 2018, https://www.rangeresources.com/range-celebrates-25-years-in-pennsylvania; "Number of Producing Gas Wells," US Energy Information Administration, Washington DC, December 30, 2021, https://www.eia.gov/dnav/ng/NG_PROD_WELLS_S1_A.htm.

30. Michael Greenstone, Janet Currie, and Kathrine Meckel, "Fracking Has Its Costs and Benefits—The Trick Is Balancing Them," *Forbes*, February 20, 2018, https://www.forbes.com/sites/ucenergy/2018/02/20/fracking-has-its-costs-and-benefits-the-trick-is-balancing-them; Shell, "Pennsylvania Petrochemicals Complex," accessed January 1, 2022, https://www.shell.com/about-us/major-projects/pennsylvania-petrochemicals-complex.html; "Shell Cracker Project Dominates PRA 2016 'Scorecard,'" *Observer Reporter* (Washington County, PA), April 6, 2017.

31. Reid Frazier, "Study Finds Methane Leaks in PA Are Much Higher than State Reports," *StateImpact Pennsylvania* (blog), May 14, 2020, https://stateimpact.npr.org/pennsylvania/2020/05/14/study-finds-methane-leaks-in-pa-are-much-higher-than-state-reports; Josh Fox, dir., *Gasland: Can You Light Your Water on Fire?*, film, Docurama, New York, 2010; Eliza Griswold, *Amity and Prosperity: One Family and the Fracturing of America* (New York: Farrar, Straus and Giroux, 2018); Iulia Gheorghiu, "Industry Groups Urge Pennsylvania GOP to Avoid Shale Tax," *Morning Consult* (blog), August 9, 2017, https://morningconsult.com/2017/08/09/industry-groups-shale-tax-concerns-up-coming-pa-house-vote.

32. Intentional and unintentional leaks from the system are still not fully accounted for and could represent a significant contribution to climate change: Neela Banerjee, "Far More Methane Leaking at Oil, Gas Sites in Pennsylvania than Reported," *Inside Climate News* (blog), February 16, 2018, https://insideclimatenews.org/news/16022018/methane-leaks-oil-natural-gas-data-global-warming-pennsylvania-edf-study.

33. Donald Giles and Kenneth Wolensky, "Harnessing the Power of the Wind: A Contemporary Use for a Historic Energy Source," *Pennsylvania Heritage*, Fall 2009, https://paheritage.wpengine.com/article/harnessing-power-wind-contemporary-historic-energy-source; Kelly Flanigan, "New Report Shows Pennsylvania Lags behind in Renewable Energy Development, despite Nationwide Growth," press release, PennEnvironment, Philadelphia, October 27, 2020, https://pennenvironment.org/news/pae/new-report-shows-pennsylvania-lags-behind-renewable-energy-development-despite-nationwide.

34. Jon Hurdle, "Pa. Regulator Says Shale Gas Drilling Method Safe," Reuters, October 1, 2010, https://www.reuters.com/article/us-pennsylvania-natgas-hanger-idUKTRE6903VG20101001; Reid Frazier, "Pa. Grand Jury Report on Fracking: DEP Failed to Protect Public Health," *StateImpact Pennsylvania* (blog), June 25, 2020, https://stateimpact.npr.org/pennsylvania/2020/06/25/pa-grand-jury-report-on-fracking-dep-failed-to-protect-peoples-health.

35. James Shortle, David Abler, Seth Blumsack, and Robert Crane, et al., "Pennsylvania Climate Impact Assessment: Report to the Department of Environmental Protection," Environment and Natural Resources Institute, Pennsylvania State University, University Park, June 29, 2009, 7–10.

36. "Pennsylvania Climate Impacts Assessment 2021," report, Pennsylvania Department of Environmental Protection, Harrisburg, May 2021, 5, 42; "In Pa., Climate Change Threatens the State Tree, Bird and Fish," StateImpact Pennsylvania, WHYY, May 10, 2023, https://whyy.org/articles/climate-change-threatens-pennsylvania-trees-birds-fish-native-species.

37. "Pennsylvania Climate Impacts Assessment 2021"; Charles Thompson, "Pa.'s Participation in Regional Cap-and-Trade Program Gets a Push from State Board," *Pennlive*, July 13, 2021, https://www.pennlive.com/news/2021/07/pas-participation-in-regional-cap-and-trade-program-gets-a-push-from-state-board-its-a-cornerstone-of-gov-wolfs-climate-change-policy.html.

38. Brett Sholtis, "Three Mile Island Nuclear Power Plant Shuts Down," National Public Radio, September 20, 2019, https://www.npr.org/2019/09/20/762762962/three-mile-island-nuclear-power-plant-shuts-down.

Conclusion

1. Wesley Robinson, "DCNR Celebrates Grand Opening of Kury Point, Legacy of PA Environmental Rights Amendment at Shikellamy State Park," *Pennsylvania Pressroom*, August 26, 2021, http://paenvironmentdaily.blogspot.com/2021/08/dcnr-celebrates-grand-opening-of-kury.html.

2. *Robinson Township, Washington County, PA et al. v. Commonwealth of Pennsylvania*, no. J-127A-D-2012, Supreme Court of Pennsylvania, Middle District (2012); John Dernbach, "The Pennsylvania Supreme Court's *Robinson Township* Decision: A Step Back for Marcellus Shale, a Step Forward for Environmental Rights and the Public Trust," *Widener Environmental Law Center* (blog), December 31, 2013, http://blogs.law.widener.edu/envirolawcenter/2013/12/21/the-pennsylvania-supreme-courts-robinson-township-decision-a-step-back-for-marcellus-shale-a-step-forward-for-article-i-section-27; John C. Dernbach, Kenneth Kristl, and James R. May, "Recognition of Environmental Rights for Pennsylvania Citizens: *Pennsylvania Environmental Defense Foundation v. Commonwealth of Pennsylvania*," Social Science Research Network Scholarly Paper, Rochester, NY, March 9, 2018.

3. Charles Thompson, "Pa.'s Participation in Regional Cap-and-Trade Program Gets a Push from State Board," *Pennlive*, July 13, 2021, https://www.pennlive.com/news/2021/07/pas-participation-in-regional-cap-and-trade-program-gets-a-push-from-state-board-its-a-cornerstone-of-gov-wolfs-climate-change-policy.html; An-Li Herring, "Wolf Trumpets Investments In Aliquippa as the Former Steel Town Braces for Cracker Plant Opening," WESA Radio, August 12, 2021, https://www.wesa.fm/politics-government/2021-08-12/wolf-trumpets-investments-in-aliquippa-as-the-former-steel-town-braces-for-cracker-plant-opening.

4. Rachel Wrigley, Wesley Robinson, and Neil Shader, "Wolf Administration Celebrates Ira Reynolds Riverfront Park Ribbon Cutting," *Pennsylvania Pressroom*, September 21, 2021, https://www.einpresswire.com/article/551961146/wolf-administration-celebrates-ira-reynolds-riverfront-park-ribbon-cutting.

5. On the history of hiking in Pennsylvania, see Silas Chamberlin, *On the Trail: A History of American Hiking* (New Haven: Yale University Press, 2016).

INDEX

Page numbers in italics refer to illustrations.

tourism, 40, 62, 70, 101
trails, nonmotorized, 15, 63, 101, 109–110; rail trails, 94, 97–98
Trollope, Frances, 34, 40

urban renewal, 69–71, 96–97

Valley Forge, 24–25, 123n25; state park, 47, 57, 63, 100

Washington, D.C., 61, 90
Washington, George, 23–26
water: for drinking, 34, 40, 48–51, 53–54, 56, 59, 64; pollution, 20–21, 47–51, 64–68, 70–75, 82–83, 92, 99; as power source, 18, 20, 31–32, 35, 39, 41. *See also* acid mine drainage; fracking
Weiser, Conrad, 13–15

Western Pennsylvania Conservancy, 77, 98
Wilderness Act, 72
wildlife, 57, 59, 72, 77, 80, 89–90, 92, 110; bounties, 9, 18, 23, 81
Wilkes-Barre, 36, 51, 59, 74
Williamsport, 42
Wilmington, Delaware, 4, 31
wind energy, 102–104
Wirt, George, 57–58
Wissahickon Creek, 20, 35, 56, 77
Works Progress Administration (WPA), 63–65
Worrell, James, 56
Wyoming Valley, 26, 29, 74. *See also* coal: anthracite

Zahniser, Howard, 72
Ziegler, Arthur, 98

Allen Dieterich-Ward is Professor of History and Director of The Graduate School at Shippensburg University. He is the author of *Beyond Rust: Metropolitan Pittsburgh and the Fate of Industrial America*, which won the Arline Custer Memorial Award for Best Book in Mid-Atlantic History.